DIS... ...R

C000177153

1 Find a time when you can read the Bible each day

2 Find a place where you can be quiet and think

4 Ask God to help you understand what you read

3 Grab your Bible and a pencil or pen

5 Read today's Discover page and Bible bit

6 Pray about what you have read and learned

We want to...

- Explain the Bible clearly to you
- Help you enjoy your Bible
- Encourage you to turn to Jesus
- Help Christians follow Jesus

Discover stands for...

- Total commitment to God's Word, the Bible
- Total commitment to getting its message over to you

Team Discover

Martin Cole, Nicole Carter, Rachel Jones, Kirsty McAllister, Alison Mitchell, André Parker, Ben Woodcraft

Discover is published by The Good Book Company, Blenheim House, 1 Blenheim Rd, Epsom, Surrey, KT19 9AP, UK.

Tel: 0333 123 0880; Email: discover@thegoodbook.co.uk UK: thegoodbook.co.uk

North America: thegoodbook.com Australia: thegoodbook.com.au NZ: thegoodbook.co.nz

How to use Discover

Here at Discover, we want you at home to get the most out of reading the Bible. It's how God speaks to us today. And He's got loads of top things to say.

We use the New International Version (NIV) of the Bible. You'll find that the NIV and New King James Version are best for doing the puzzles in Discover.

The Bible has 66 different books in it. So if the notes say…

Read Luke 1 v 1

…turn to the contents page of your Bible and look down the list of books to see what page Genesis begins on. Turn to that page.

"Luke 1 v 1" means you need to go to chapter 1 of Luke, and then find verse 1 of chapter 1 (the verse numbers are the tiny ones). Then jump in and read it!

Here's some other stuff you might come across…

WEIRD WORDS

Trangletof
These boxes explain baffling words or phrases we come across in the Bible.

Think!

This bit usually has a tricky personal question on what you've been reading about.

Action!

Challenges you to put what you've read into action.

Wow!

This section contains a gobsmacking fact that sums up what you've been reading about.

Pray!

Gives you ideas for prayer. Prayer is talking to God. Don't be embarrassed! You can pray in your head if you want to. God still hears you! Even if there isn't a Pray! symbol, it's a good idea to pray about what you've read anyway.

Coming up in Issue 9...

Luke: Life with Jesus

Have you ever wondered how we can be sure about Jesus?

Luke was a doctor and a historian who lived almost 2000 years ago — and he wanted people to be sure about Jesus. So he set about investigating the evidence and interviewing the people who knew Jesus personally. Then Luke recorded it all carefully and clearly in a biography of Jesus that we have in our Bibles today — Luke's Gospel.

So we'll read all about Mary and Joseph's strange birth announcement, the time Jesus got lost in the ~~supermarket~~ temple, and loads of the things Jesus did and taught once He grew up. Luke's book is full of amazing stuff because it's about an amazing man — God's Son, Jesus Christ!

Joshua: Follow the leader

Next we march into the book of Joshua. It's all about God leading His people (the Israelites) into Canaan, the wonderful land He had promised them.

The book is named after the guy who was in charge of Israel at the time: Joshua. But the Israelites (and all the other nations around them) will see who's really in charge: God!

This Bible book is full of guts and gore, blood and battles. But it makes a really important point — God is a powerful promise keeper, and it's GREAT to be one of His people!

Romans: Right with God

Ever asked questions like these...?

How can I know if God really loves me?

Can I just keep sinning if God's going to forgive me anyway?

How did the Romans cut their hair?*

The book of Romans has answers to (almost) all these questions and loads more! It's a letter written by a church leader called Paul to a group of Christians in Rome, Italy.

We pick up the letter in chapter 5. In the first part, Paul explains how absolutely *everyone* has done wrong. Which leaves us wondering: how can we possibly get right with God? Read Romans and find out!

* With a pair of *Caesars*!

**Ready to start reading?
Then let's turn over...**

Luke: Life with Jesus

Luke
1 v 1-4

How long to go until Christmas?

Is it days, weeks or months away?!

WEIRD WORDS

Undertaken
Decided

Fulfilled
Old Testament prophecies that came true in Jesus' life

Servants of the word
People dedicated to telling others about Jesus

Orderly account
Reliable book about Jesus

In this issue of Discover we're going to start reading Luke's Gospel — and it all begins with the Christmas story!

Luke's book isn't big on tinsel or baubles, but it *is* full of the awesome news about Jesus. And that means there's no one right time of year to read it!

Fantastic fact 1

Gospel means good news. Luke is telling us the good news about Jesus and why He came to earth.

Read the start of Luke's Gospel in Luke 1 v 1-4

Luke is writing to a guy called Theophilus to tell him all about Jesus and the incredible things Jesus did and said.

Fantastic fact 2

Theophilus means *friend of God*. Theophilus wanted to know more about Jesus. Friends of God want to know all about Jesus!

Complete what Luke says in verses 3-4 by adding every missing i, c and t.

I have __arefully
__nvest__ga__ed
every__h__ng from the
beg__nn__ng. I decided __o
wr__te an orderly a__ __ount
for you so __hat you may
know the __erta__nty of the
__hings you have
been __aught.

Luke carefully investigated what he'd heard about Jesus. Luke's book is a collection of the amazing things he found out about Jesus. He wanted Theophilus to be certain about who Jesus was. We can learn all about Jesus from Luke's book and be certain about who Jesus is too!

Think!

Are you a *friend of God*, like Theophilus was? Do you want to learn more about Jesus?

Pray!

Ask God to teach you loads of new things about Jesus as you read Luke's book. Ask God to help you be CERTAIN of the truth about Jesus.

2

We're reading about the start of Jesus' life Luke's book.

WEIRD WORDS

Judea
Area around Jerusalem

Priestly division of Abijah
One of the 24 groups of priests

Righteous
Living God's way

Observing
Keeping

Blamelessly
Without fault

Conceive
Become pregnant

Golden oldies

Today we meet two important characters. You may not have heard of them...

Read Luke 1 v 5-7

All of today's answers can be found in the wordsearch.

Z	F	V	C	C	E	Z	O	A
E	L	I	Z	A	B	E	T	H
C	O	M	M	A	N	D	S	N
H	P	D	Q	L	K	L	G	R
A	B	S	P	R	I	E	S	T
R	T	I	K	Y	O	F	J	D
I	N	G	U	S	L	T	H	X
A	C	H	I	L	D	R	E	N
H	G	T	E	B	Z	P	J	S

Luke tells us about...

Z_____

and his wife

E_____

What does Luke tell us about them?

Zechariah was a

p_____ (v5)

They both lived good lives in God's s_____ (v6).
They kept God's

c_____ (v6)

They were serious about living God's way and obeying Him.

Think!

Do you live in a way that pleases God? Do you obey what you learn in the Bible?

Action!

Grab a notebook. Create a section called **What I've learned**. Every time you read your Bible, write down what you've learned from it.

Then make a section called **What I'll do**. There write down what you're going to do about what you've learned.

Once a week, read the two sections. Talk to God about what you've learned and what you'll do about it.

Elizabeth couldn't have c_____ (v7). They were both o_____ (v7).

In those days it was a disgrace for a woman to have no children. They were elderly so it seemed too late for them. But nothing is impossible for God, as we'll find out tomorrow.

Pray!

Ask God to help you learn loads from the Gospel of Luke and act on what you learn.

Brilliant baby bulletin

**Luke
1 v 8-17**

Yesterday we met Zechariah and Elizabeth. They loved God and obeyed His laws. But they had been unable to have children.

Read Luke 1 v 8-13

Now cross out the wrong answers.

Zechariah was chosen to go into the tent/temple/turtle and burn insects/incense (v9). Amazingly, an angel/demon/prophet of the Lord appeared (v11). Zechariah was brave/scared. The angel said: *"Don't be afraid, your whisper/prayer has been heard. Elizabeth will have a bun/son/daughter. You must call him Jim/John."*

That's amazing! They must have given up the hope of ever having a baby. But now God was answering their prayers in an amazing way!

Remember — God doesn't always answer prayers when **we** think He

will. We sometimes have to wait a long time for an answer.

This would be a very special son.

Read verses 14-17

Many people will be happy/sad when he is born (v14) for he'll be a great man in the Lord's sight/smell/hearing (v15). He will never drink cola/wine (v15) and he'll be filled with the Holy Spirit. He will bring many people of Egypt/Israel back to God! (v16) He will get them ready/greeny/browny for the Lord (v17).

Wow!

Hundreds of years earlier, God promised to send a messenger to tell His people *"Get ready for the Rescuer"*. God kept His promise. John would be that messenger, preparing the way for Jesus.

Pray!

Thank God for sending John the Baptist. Thank God that He answers our prayers and always keeps His promises.

WEIRD WORDS

Burn incense
Burn a powder that makes a sweet smell at the altar where people brought gifts to God

Rejoice
Be really happy!

Fermented
Alcoholic

Holy Spirit
The Holy Spirit is God. He helped prophets to speak words from God

The righteous
People who've had their sins forgiven by God

4

An angel visited Zechariah and told him that he and his wife were going to have a baby.

God had answered their prayers!

WEIRD WORDS

In seclusion
On her own, away from people

Favour
Love and kindness

Disgrace
Elizabeth's shame of not being able to have children

Dumbstruck

Which of these would you believe? × or ✓

• The planet Jupiter is made of marshmallow

• All schools are being closed down forever

• Your mum will be the next Queen of England

Zechariah knew that Elizabeth wasn't able to have children.

But the angel Gabriel has just told him that she will have a son.

Do you think he will believe the angel?

Yes/No/Maybe _____

Read Luke 1 v 18-22

Zechariah didn't believe the angel. Gabriel was God's messenger, so that's the same as not believing God Himself!

So Gabriel made Zechariah unable to speak until God's promise came true and the baby was born.

Wow!

We can trust what God says to us. He doesn't usually send angels to speak to us! Instead, God speaks to us when we read His Word in the Bible. We can trust it completely.

Think & pray 1

Do you find it easy to believe the Bible? And easy to do what it says? Ask God to help you **understand**, **believe** and **obey** what you read in the Bible.

Read verses 23-25
What did Elizabeth say (v25)?
Go forward one letter to find out.

___ ___ ___   ___ ___ ___ ___
S G D   K N Q C

___ ___ ___   ___ ___ ___ ___
G Z R   C N M D

___ ___ ___ ___   ___ ___ ___   ___ ___
S G H R   E N Q   L D

Elizabeth knew that the baby was from the Lord. She thanked and praised God loads.

Think & pray 2

Do you notice when God answers your prayers? Think back to prayers you've made that God has answered. Now thank Him!

5

Brilliant baby bulletin 2

**Luke
1 v 26-33**

God made it possible for Elizabeth to have a baby!

Now the story switches to Elizabeth's relative Mary...

Read Luke 1 v 26-31

What a shock for Mary! She was going to have a baby too! The angel told her to call her baby **Jesus**. *Use the code to discover what the name* **Jesus** *means.*

This baby would be even more special than Elizabeth's son! God sent Jesus into the world to **save** people from the results of sin!

Read verses 32-33

What else did Gabriel tell Mary about Jesus?

He will be called
_ _ _ _ **of the**

Jesus is God's Son,
born as a human baby!

His kingdom will

Jesus would be King of God's people. And not just the Israelites, but all of God's people, Christians. They will live in heaven with Jesus as their King forever!

Pray!

Thank God for sending His Son to earth — the best Christmas present ever!

For the free e-booklet *Why did Jesus come?* email discover@thegoodbook.co.uk or check out www.thegoodbook.co.uk/contact-us to find our UK mailing address.

For the free e-booklet *Why did Jesus come?* email discover@thegoodbook.co.uk or check out www.thegoodbook.co.uk/contact-us to find our UK mailing address.

WEIRD WORDS

Virgin
Someone who hasn't had sex, because it's wrong to before marriage

David
Great king who defeated Goliath

Conceive
Become pregnant

The Most High
God

Reign
Rule as King

Jacob's descendants
The Israelites, God's special people

A	D	E	G	H	I	M	N	O	R	S	T	V

6

Luke
1 v 34-38

The angel Gabriel has appeared to Mary and told her that she will have a baby.

Mary's baby would be God's Son, Jesus — the greatest person that ever lived!

WEIRD WORDS

Virgin
Someone who hasn't had sex

The Most High
God

Conceive
Become pregnant

Sixth month
of being pregnant

Pregnant pause

How do you think Mary felt about this news?

_____

_____

_____

Read Luke 1 v 34

Mary wasn't yet married to Joseph. It seemed impossible to her that she could be pregnant.

Read verses 35-37

Who would make it possible for Mary to have a baby (v35)?

The H_____ S_____

The Holy Spirit is the Helper who God gives to all Christians to help them serve Him. Here, the Holy Spirit miraculously caused Mary to be pregnant!

Does that sound impossible? Well, check out something else that Gabriel said to Mary. Find it by taking **every second letter**, starting with the **F** at the top.

F _ _
_ _ _ _ _ _
_ _
_ _ _ _ _ _ _
_ _ _ _
_ _ _

Wow!

Some Bibles say: "No word from God will ever fail". They both mean the same thing. Nothing is impossible for God! When He says He'll do something, He will. Because He can do anything. He can use unknown people like Mary (and you and me!) to serve Him in amazing ways!

Read verse 38

Mary **believed** what the angel said, **trusted** God to keep His promise and wanted to **obey** God, whatever He commanded.

Pray!

Dear God, please help me to **believe** Your words in the Bible. Help me to **trust** You more. And please help me to **obey** whatever You want me to do. Amen.

1

I did well in my exam!

We're going on holiday to Hawaii!

What do you do when you have some good news?

You share it!

WEIRD WORDS

Judea
Area around Jerusalem

Fulfil
Keep

The bump jumps for joy!

Mary would have a baby who will be God's Son! Mary wanted to share her great news with her relative Elizabeth. The angel had told her that Elizabeth was pregnant too, so they could share in their happiness and excitement.

Read Luke 1 v 39-41

*What **two** amazing things happened?*

1. The b_____ leaped in Elizabeth's womb!

The baby inside Elizabeth was John, who would grow up to tell people about Jesus.

Even as an unborn baby he was excited about Jesus!!

Do YOU get excited about Jesus? Do you want to tell others about Him?

2. Elizabeth was filled with the H_____ S_____

The Holy Spirit points people to Jesus. That's how Elizabeth knew Mary was to be Jesus' mum. The Holy Spirit helps us to understand the Bible and learn more about Jesus.

Read verses 42-45

What word does Elizabeth repeat several times?

B__ __ __ __ __ __

That means God is pleased with Mary and has given her a great gift (Jesus). Mary was blessed in **three** ways...

1. Blessed are you among w_____ (v42)

Mary was specially chosen out of all women to give birth to Jesus!

2. Blessed is the c_____ you will bear (v42)

Mary's baby would be the most important person that ever lived — Jesus!

3. Blessed is she who b_____ what the Lord said to her (v45)

Mary was blessed because she believed that God would keep His great promise to let her be Jesus' mother.

Pray!

Ask God to help you believe what you read in the Bible about Jesus. Ask God to get you excited about Jesus!

8

Pregnant praise

Luke 1 v 46-56

WEIRD WORDS

My soul glorifies
I praise God with everything I've got

Spirit rejoices
I'm really happy!

Saviour
Rescuer

Mindful
Aware

Humble state
Mary was unknown and unimportant, yet God used her

Holy
Pure and perfect

Mercy
Incredible forgiveness

Mary is going to give birth to God's Son! She is so excited that she praises and thanks God loads!

Read Luke 1 v 46-50

What great truths about God does Mary mention? Use the words down the centre.

God is...

my S____________ (v47)

God wants to rescue us.

m__________ (v49)

He is stronger and more powerful than anyone or anything else!

full of m__________ (v50)

We deserve to be punished for sinning against God. But God wants to rescue us from this punishment, even though we deserve it! That's mercy!

Read verses 51-56

Mary talks about some of the great things God has done.

good helped hungry Israel lifted mercy mighty proud rulers Saviour thrones

God has...

scattered p_________ people (v51) and brought down r________ from their th_______ (v52)

God is angry with people who think they don't need Him.

l__________ up the humble (v52) filled the h__________ with g_______ things (v53)

God loves people who others look down on. He even uses them to serve Him in great ways. Like Mary!

h__________ his servant I__________ (v54)

God looked after His people, the Israelites, keeping His promises to them. And God looks after His people (Christians) today too!

Mary is praising God because He is so good to those who trust Him and serve Him.

Pray!

What great things can you praise and thank God for?

____

____

____

____

Now do it as you talk to God.

9

Luke
1 v 57-66

If you had a new baby brother and could choose his name, what would it be?

_____

Look who's talking!

In Bible times, people named their children after their relations. So it looked as if Elizabeth's baby would be named after her husband...

Z_____

It even had a great meaning — *God has remembered.*

Read Luke 1 v 57-61

What did Elizabeth say (v60)?

> **He is to be called** _____

Her family were not happy about this. So they asked Zechariah (who the angel had made unable to speak).

Read verses 62-64

What did Zechariah write?

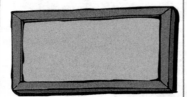

Do you remember what the angel had said to Zechariah? Find it in **Luke 1 v 13.**

> **Your wife**
> **E**_____ **will bear you a s_____ and you are to call him J_____.**

God had told them to call him **John**. It means *"the Lord is gracious"* — God gives people far more than they deserve. So Elizabeth and Zechariah **obeyed God** and called their son John.

Think!

What has God done for you that you didn't deserve?

_____

_____

_____

God gave this baby a special name because He had a special plan for John's life.

Read verses 65-66

What does the last sentence of verse 66 say?

The Lord's _____

_____

God was with John and would help John to serve Him.

Pray!

Do you want to serve God? Ask God to be with you, helping you serve Him with the way you live. Praise and thank Him for doing what you wrote down under Think!

**Luke
1 v 67-75**

Thank you God!

The story is gathering pace. God answered Zechariah and Elizabeth's prayers by giving them a son called John. It's Zechariah's turn to praise and thank God now!

Read Luke 1 v 67-75

Each sentence below sums up one of the verses you've just read. Find the right verse number for each one and shade in that verse number on the grid. Sometimes you'll need to shade in more than one square.

Praise God! He has come and redeemed His people	75	68	68	68	68	68
Long ago, the prophets said it would happen like this	73	68	71	70	74	71
He has sent us a Saviour who is from King David's family	70	75	75	69	73	72
He promised to show mercy to our ancestors and keep His covenant	75	73	74	72	70	73
God has kept His promise (oath) to Abraham	71	70	74	73	69	68
We'll be saved from our enemies and those who hate us	69	72	75	71	68	73
God will rescue us so that we can serve Him without fear	74	68	68	74	69	72
...and live holy, righteous lives all our days	68	75	75	71	70	69

The shaded squares should form a letter. No prizes for guessing who the letter stands for...

J__ __ __ __

WEIRD WORDS

Prophesied
Spoke the truth from God

Redeemed
Bought back, rescued

Horn of salvation
That means strong rescuer. That's Jesus!

House of David
David's family

Holy prophets
God's messengers

Covenant
Agreement that God made with the Israelites

Holiness and righteousness
Living God's way

Zechariah thanked God for sending baby Jesus. Jesus was the Rescuer who God had promised would save His people. Now read the sentences and verses 67-75 again. ➡

Action!

We can thank God for those things too! Pick two or three of the sentences and thank God for those amazing things.

Future shock

Luke 1 v 76-80

Zechariah has been thanking and praising God for giving him a son.

But what will baby John be like when he grows up?

> This boy will win an Olympic gold medal. He'll live in France with his wife and three children.

Imagine a father predicting that about his newborn son. You'd think he was out of his mind.

But read what Zechariah said about baby John...

Read Luke 1 v 76-80

Zechariah's prediction came true. But that's not really surprising, because it came from the Holy Spirit (see v67).

To see how God would use John, fill in the missing letters.

John would be God's p__ophet (v76).

He would prepare people for the Lord J__sus (v76).

Jesus would rescue __eople by forgiving their sins (v77), because God had m__rcy on them (v78).

Jesus came to people living in the dark__ess of their sin (v79)...

...to shine on them the ligh__ of His forgiving love.

Take the letters you stuck in the gaps and put them into the speech bubble below, in the same order. The word sums up the main message John would bring the people...

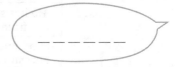

That means **turn away from your wrong ways**. John would tell people to turn away from sin and start living God's way. Then they'd be ready to follow Jesus!

Action!

What wrong things do you need to turn away from, so you can serve Jesus better?

_____

_____

_____

Ask God to help you turn your back on doing those things and start living His way more.

A child is born

**Luke
2 v 1-7**

What's the longest distance you've ever walked?

_____

Mary and Joseph are about to go on a looooong journey — 68 miles!

WEIRD WORDS

Decree
Command

Census
Counting all the people in the Roman empire

Town of David
Bethlehem, where King David was born

House and line
Family

Manger
Animal food trough

Read Luke 2 v 1-5

Caesar Augustus, the Roman emperor, wanted to know how many people lived in his Roman empire. So everyone had to go to their home town to be counted. Then the Romans would know how much tax they should get.

So Joseph took pregnant Mary to his family's town of Bethlehem.

Brainstorm!

Ever done a brainstorm? It just means writing down anything that comes into your brain about a subject.

So if I say CHRISTMAS, what do you think of? Write down the first things you think of in the thought bubble below.

There are loads of things to get excited about around Christmas time. Maybe you're excited already! But here's the number one reason to be excited...

Read verses 6-7

Wow!

Christmas is all about a real person who came to earth from heaven. He slept in an animal trough, not a palace. But this was God's Son, the most important person ever! Christmas is all about JESUS!

JESUS CAME TO EARTH TO RESCUE SINFUL PEOPLE LIKE US

That's what Christmas is about — and that's a truth that changes our lives all year round, whether it's January or December!

Pray!

Thank God for sending His Son Jesus into the world!

Here is the news...

13

Luke 2 v 8-14

There's loads of great news at Christmas time: presents, fantastic food, surprises...

...and there's even better news than that!

WEIRD WORDS

Town of David
Bethlehem

Saviour
Rescuer

Messiah
The King who God promised would rescue His people

Heavenly host
Loads and loads of angels

Read Luke 2 v 8-12

What was the great news (v12)? Fill in the missing vowels please!

> T__d__y in the t__wn of
> D__v__d a S__v__ __ __r
> has been b__rn to y__ __:
> he is the M__ss__ __h,
> the L__rd.

That's brilliant news! Jesus had been born, and He was the Messiah, sent by God to rescue His people!

Who heard the good news first?

- **Emperor Caesar** ☐
- **Chief priests** ☐
- **News reporters** ☐
- **Ordinary shepherds** ☐

There was nothing special about these shepherds. They were just ordinary guys. The good news about Jesus is for **ordinary people** like us!

That's what the angel said too!

Check out his words in verse 10.

> **I bring you good news...**
> It's fantastic news that God sent His Son to earth! To rescue us from all our sin, so we can be right with God.

> **...that will cause great joy...**
> Are you excited by this good news? Christians will want to praise and thank God for giving them the amazing gift of His Son!

> **...for all the people**
> From kings and queens down to poor shepherds. Anyone can trust in Jesus to forgive them for their wrongs!

The angels got excited too!

Read verses 13-14

Pray!

Thank God for the great news about Jesus. Ask Him to help you tell more people this great news.

Shepherd spy

Follow both flow charts to work through today's Bible bit.
Circle the correct answers as you go along.

Loads of angels appeared to some shepherds, giving them **"good news that will cause great joy for all the people"**.

The good news was that Jesus had been born nearby.

Time to spy out this amazing baby!

1
Read Luke 2 v 15-16
What did the shepherds do when they heard the good news about Jesus?

| Carried on working | Went to find Jesus |

2
Read verses 17-18
What did the shepherds do when they found Jesus?

| Kept it to themselves | Told anyone who would listen |

3
Read verses 19-20
How much of what the angels told the shepherds was true?

| All | Some | None |

4
Did they praise God that they'd found Jesus?

| Yes | No |

1
You have heard the good news about Jesus — that He came to earth so that He could die on the cross and take the punishment we deserve. *How should you respond to this good news?*

| Carry on living for yourself | Go to Jesus and tell Him you'll live for Him |

2
If you have turned to Jesus, what should you do?

| Keep quiet about it | Tell people the good news |

3
How much of what the Bible says about Jesus is true?

| None | Some | All |

4
If you've had your sins forgiven by Jesus, will you praise and thank God?

| Yes | No |

WEIRD WORDS

Glorifying
Praising God, giving Him the honour and glory He deserves

Pray! Go on then! Talk to God and tell Him how you feel. And ask Him to help you spread the news about Jesus!

Law and order

Luke
2 v 21-24

What does 'THE LAW' make you think of? Circle any of these and add your own.

police court judge

terrorists

rules teachers

We should obey the law of the country we live in (see 1 Peter 2 v 13-14). But there's an even more important law than that. It appears twice in Luke 2 v 23-24.

The law of _____

Christians obey God's law.

That means obeying what we're taught in the Bible.

Read Luke 2 v 21-24

Law fact 1

Some of the laws that Jewish people obeyed were picture lessons to them. They were specifically for God's people **before** Jesus, so we aren't expected to keep them now.

Example

Mary and Joseph had to offer a sacrifice of doves or pigeons to God (v24). But when Jesus died, the sacrifice of His death was enough to satisfy God. So now, Christians don't need to offer sacrifices to God. Jesus has done it for us!

Law fact 2

There are still plenty of Old Testament laws we should obey. For example, the Ten Commandments teach us how to live God's way. So we should obey them!

Did Mary and Joseph...

- give their son the name the angel gave them (v21)? _____
- obey God's law to circumcise Jesus (v21)? _____
- obey God's law to take Jesus to the temple (v22)? _____
- obey God's law about sacrifices (v24)? _____

Action!

Which of God's laws do you need to try harder to obey? (The 10 Commandments can be found in Exodus 20 v 1-17.)

_____

_____

_____

Now ask God to help you!

Luke
2 v 25-35

Simeon says

Read Luke 2 v 25-26

Joseph and Mary took baby Jesus to God's temple to show that Jesus' life would be given to serving God. Old Simeon had been waiting all his life to meet the Messiah (Christ) and now he did!

Read verses 27-35

Use the backwards word pool to reveal what Simeon said about Jesus.

delaever   dlihc

learsl   noitavlas

selitneG   seye   sthguoht

straeh   thgil   yrolg

My e_____ have seen your

s_____ (v30)

God sent Jesus to rescue people from their sinful lives.

Jesus is a l_____ for

revelation to the G_____

and the g_____ of God's

people I_____ (v32)

God sent Jesus to rescue His people, the Israelites. But Jesus also rescues Gentiles (non-Israelites) too! **Anyone** can have their sins forgiven!

This c_____ will cause

the falling and rising of

many in Israel (v34) so

that the t_____ of

many h_____ will be

r_____ (v35)

Jesus knows what's in our thoughts and in our hearts — what we're really like. Everyone who trusts Jesus' death to save them will be forgiven. Everyone who rejects Him will be punished in hell.

Pray!

Read through those three bits of bold writing again. What have you learned about Jesus today?

_____

_____

_____

Spend time thanking God for the amazing things Simeon has taught you about Jesus.

WEIRD WORDS

Righteous and devout
Devoted to God, living His way

Consolation of Israel
God sending the Messiah to comfort His people

Sovereign
In control of everything

Salvation
Rescue

Revelation
Revealing the truth

Marvelled
Were amazed

Destined
God says this will definitely happen

Luke
2 v 36-40

Yesterday we met Simeon, who told us great things about Jesus.

Today we meet elderly Anna...

WEIRD WORDS

Prophet/ Prophetess
God's messenger

Fasting
Going without food to spend more time worshipping God

Redemption of Jerusalem
God rescuing His people

Grace of God
God was looking after Him

Anna list

Read Luke 2 v 36-40

What an amazing woman! Anna was 84 and she still continued to serve God with great enthusiasm!

We can learn so much from older Christians. They've been serving God much longer than we have. Try chatting to an elderly Christian at church this week. Ask them how they've stuck at it for sooooo long.

Go back one letter (B=A) to find **three things** that show Anna loved God.

X P S T I J Q Q F E

God day and night

Every minute of her day was given to serving God, living to please Him.

G B T U J O H

That means going without food so she could spend extra time with God.

Q S B Z J O H

Anna talked to God all the time. People who love God usually spend lots of time praying.

Action!

What can you give up so you have more time to pray?

(It doesn't have to be food!)

_____

_____

Why not give it a go?

What else did Anna do (v38)?

U P M E   Q F P Q M F

B C P V U   K F T V T

People who love God do all of those things: they try to worship God with their whole lives; they put other things aside so they can spend longer in prayer; they tell other people about Jesus — all because he's so amazing!.

Pray!

Which one of those things do you need God to help you with?

_____

Spend extra time talking to God about it right now.

Missing parents

**Luke
2 v 41-52**

*Ever lost someone
when you're out
and about in a
busy place?*

*It can be pretty
scary, can't it?*

WEIRD WORDS

Custom
What they did every
year

Anxiously
Worriedly

Nazareth
Town where Jesus
and His family lived

Stature
Size and strength

Read Luke 2 v 41-45

Cross out the wrong answers.

**When Jesus was two/
twelve/twenty, He went
with His parrot/parents to
Jerusalem for the Pushover/
Passover Feast. After the
feast, Jesus stayed in
Jerusalem/Jericho/Jellyfish.
After a day/week/month of
travelling, His parents began
to look/cook for Him. When
they couldn't find Jesus,
they went back to Jerusalem
to search for Him.**

Read verses 46-50

**After three days they found
Jesus in the tennis/temple
courts with the teachers/
doctors/nurses, asking
them questions. Everyone
was bored/amazed at His
understanding of the Bible.**

*Where did Jesus tell His mother He'd
been all that time (v49)?*

In my F_____

Wow!

Jesus had been in His Father's
house — God's temple. In his book
about Jesus, Luke wants his readers
to understand that Jesus is **GOD'S
SON**, sent to earth to rescue people.

Jesus was questioning and listening
to experts on the Old Testament. He
longed to learn from God's Word.

Action!

How about you? Will you try to read
the Bible more often (not just with
Discover)?

Will you listen more to people who
teach you from the Bible? Will you
ask more questions?

Read verses 51-52

Don't think that Jesus staying
behind in Jerusalem means it's OK
to disobey your parents. After that,
Jesus obeyed His parents fully (v51)
and so should you!

Pray!

Ask God to help you be like Jesus:
reading the Bible and learning
how to live God's way.

Joshua: Follow the leader

**Joshua
1 v 1-5**

Welcome to the book of Joshua.

It's all about God leading His people (the Israelites) into Canaan, the land He had promised them.

WEIRD WORDS

Territory
The area you will live in and own

Forsake
Abandon

HISTORY FILE

Back in Genesis 12 v 1-3, God promised Abraham 3 things:

1. **Abraham's family would become a great nation.**

2. **They would live in a wonderful land.**

3. **They would be a blessing to others.**

As we begin the story of Joshua, it's 600 years since Abraham died. Have God's promises come true yet?

Promise 1 had come true. Abraham's family were a HUGE nation called the Israelites!

Promise 3 would come true when Jesus came to earth.

But **Promise 2** is about to come true! The book of Joshua is all about it.

Moses had been leading the Israelites to Canaan. But they disobeyed God and were made to wander the desert for 40 years.

Now, Moses is dead and the Israelites need someone to lead them into God's promised land...

Read Joshua 1 v 1-5

Joshua's job
Leader of God's special people — the Israelites.

What it involved
Leading the people into Canaan and conquering it. The land is currently full of fierce armies, walled cities, and giant enemies.

What else?
To believe all that God says.
To trust in God's power.
To always obey God.

*What a scary task! But look at God's encouraging words in **verse 5**! Fill in the vowels (aeiou) in the speech bubble.*

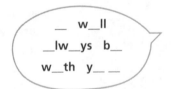

_ _ w_ll
_lw_ys b_
w_th y_ _

Pray!

Whatever the next few months hold for you, if you're a Christian, then this promise is for you too! Tell God any worries you have, and thank Him that He's always with you!

**Joshua
1 v 6-9**

Extra strong hints

God has chosen Joshua to lead the Israelites into the promised land (Canaan). It's a tough task, but God has some great advice to help Joshua...

Read Joshua 1 v 6-9

What did God say to Joshua? Cross out the words FEAR and WEAK to find out.

WEIRD WORDS

Courageous
Brave

Inherit
Get the land that
God had promised to
their ancestors

Swore
Promised

Book of the Law
God's law — how
God wants His
people to live

Meditate on it
Think about it

Prosperous
Given great things
by God

```
B E S T R F E A R O N G
A W E A K N D C F E A R O
U R A G W E A K E O U S
B_  _ _ _ _ _ _

   _ _ _

_ _ _ _ _ _ _ _ _
```

How many times does God say this in v6-9? ☐

It must be important!

Wow!

Yesterday we read that God promised always to be with Joshua. So Joshua really could be strong and brave!

God is always with all His people (Christians). So we can be strong and brave too!

Read verses 7-8 again

You might find the weird word box (on the left) helpful.

What must Joshua do with God's Word? Cross out the wrong answers.

**Ignore it   Obey it all
Don't turn away from it
Obey just the bits you like
Listen to it   Talk about it
Keep quiet about it**

Today, we have much more of God's Word than Joshua did. We have the whole Bible, to read, learn and tell others about! If we do that, God will look after us (v8)!

Action!

Let's make a start right now! Spend time learning verse 8. You'll find it helpful to write it out. Stick it where you'll keep seeing it, to help you and remind you. Ask God to help you remember these great words from the Bible.

Stay or obey?

**Joshua
1 v 10-18**

Do you go to church or a Christian group?

Do you enjoy it?

What about the people?

Do you get along with them?

All of them?!

WEIRD WORDS

Officers of the people
Leaders

The Jordan
Large river

Livestock
Animals

Rebels
Goes against

All of God's people (the Israelites) are on their way to Canaan. That's the country God has promised to give them.

But will they all stick together?

Read Joshua 1 v 10-11

It's looking good so far. But...

> **Problem!**
>
> Not everyone wanted to live in Canaan. Two and a half of the twelve tribes of Israel were going to live outside of Canaan.
>
> But Joshua still wanted their fighting men to help out in the battles, because all of God's people were in it together!

Read verses 12-15

Tricky. Would these tribes send their fighting men to help out Joshua and the rest of the Israelites?

Read verses 16-18

Follow the spiral and fill in the speech bubble.

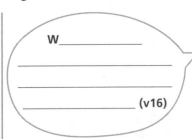

W_____
_____
_____
_____ (v16)

They promised to obey Joshua and especially to **obey God**.

Think!

Are you eager to obey God and do things His way?

And do you stick together with other Christians, helping them out when they need your help? Even ones you don't get on with so well?

We will do everything you have told us and will go where you send us

Pray!

Ask God to help you to obey Him and do things His way. Ask Him to help you be a better friend to other Christians you know. Then make sure you do something about it!

**Joshua
2 v 1-7**

Joshua is going to lead the Israelites into Canaan.

That means they'll have to cross the River Jordan and conquer the city of Jericho.

Hide and sneak

So Joshua sent two spies to cross the river and check out how well protected Jericho was.

Read Joshua 2 v 1-7

Now rearrange these blocks to tell the story in the correct order. Do it by filling in the blank blocks on the right.

Rahab tricked the spy-catchers

The King of Jericho questioned Rahab

The spy-catchers went the wrong way

The spies stayed at Rahab's place

Joshua sent two spies into Canaan

Rahab hid the spies under some plants

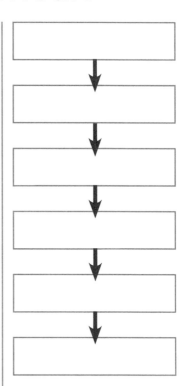

Rahab was not one of God's people, yet she helped the spies to hide. God used this unlikely person in His plans.

Wow!

Sometimes God uses the most surprising people and methods in His plans. But He is in control and always does what's best for His people.

Pray!

Thank God that His plans always work out for the good of His people.

Faith in strange places

**Joshua
2 v 8-11**

Rahab has been
helping God's
spies to hide
from the king of
Jericho.

But why did she
risk her life for
these strangers?

Time to find out...

Read Joshua 2 v 8-11

*Fill in what Rahab had heard
about God.*

> I know that the
> L_____ has given this
> l_____ to you (v8)

> The Lord dried up the
> R_____ S_____ and
> helped you escape from
> E_____ (v10)

> The Lord is in
> h_____ above and
> on the e_____ below
> (v11)

Rahab had heard how God had
been with the Israelites and done
amazing things for them. She had
learned three things about God...

So, Rahab was afraid of God and
helped God's spies to escape. But
that's not all...

Check out Hebrews 11 v 31

**Rahab had f_____
in God! She believed in
Him and trusted Him!**

1. **God is strong and
   powerful.**
2. **He is God of heaven and
   earth. That's EVERYTHING!**
3. **He's in control of
   everything that happens.**

Think!

You know even more fantastic
things about God than Rahab did!
Write some of them here:

_____

_____

_____

_____

_____

You know all this and more! So
do you believe in God? Trust
Him? Live for Him?

Pray!

Do you believe these things
about God too?
Then spend some time right
now thanking and praising God
for each one of them.

Rahab's rope trick

**Joshua
2 v 12-24**

*Rahab has
helped the spies
to hide, because
she knows that
God is on their
side.*

Read Joshua 2 v 12-13

*Go forward 2 letters (A=C, B=D,
C=E, Y=A, Z=B etc) and fill in what
Rahab said.*

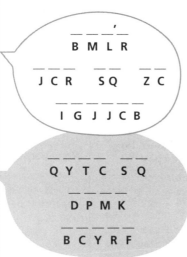

_ _ _ _ '
B M L R

_ _ _ _ _ _ _
J C R S Q Z C

_ _ _ _ _ _
I G J J C B

_ _ _ _ _ _ _
Q Y T C S Q

_ _ _ _
D P M K

_ _ _ _ _
B C Y R F

Wow, Rahab really does have faith
in God! She knows that the city of
Jericho is going to be destroyed.
And she knows that **only God** can
save her from death.

Think!

We all need to be saved too!
Everyone who has done wrong is
heading towards everlasting death.
But like Rahab, we can escape
death too...

Read verses 14-21

*What did Rahab have to do to be
rescued from death?*

Tie a _____

in the _____

When the Israelites saw this, they
would know that Rahab was on
God's side and would keep her alive.
So how do we escape the death **we**
deserve for disobeying God?

Read John 3 v 16

Wow!

To save us from death, God sent
Jesus to die in our place. If we
believe in Jesus and trust Him to
save us, then He will rescue us from
the death we deserve!

**Read Joshua 2 v 22-24 to see
how the spies escaped and what
they told Joshua...**

25

Ark and ride

The spies have told Joshua that the people of Canaan are scared of God.

Great news!

So it's time to get ready to cross the river Jordan and invade Canaan.

WEIRD WORDS

Levitical priests
Priests from the Israelite tribe of Levi

Consecrate
Make clean and ready for God, by washing in a special way

Read Joshua 3 v 1-3

What are the people supposed to follow?

What is it?!
**Ark of the covenant
(also called covenant box, and sacred chest)**

Large wooden box that had the 10 Commandments in it.

It was a big reminder that God was with His people. It also reminded them of the great promises He had made.

Quickly scan through chapters 3 and 4 of Joshua.

How many times is the ark mentioned?

Read verse 4

The people had to follow the ark. It was **God** who was leading them! He would lead them across the Jordan and lead them to victory!

Action!

As a reminder that God leads His people, write out the words of 2 Samuel 22 v 33 and stick them up where you'll see them every day.

Read verses 5-6

That means they had to wash and prepare themselves in a special way. They had to be ready for God to lead them.

Think!

How can you be more prepared to follow God? By trying to keep what you do, think and say "clean"? By spending more time praying and reading the Bible?

Ultimately, it's **Jesus** who washes us clean of our sins so that we can serve God. That's totally awesome!

Pray!

Thank God that He's leading you through life. Ask Him to help you be more prepared to follow Him.

**I counted sixteen!
It must be really important!**

26

Mission impossible?

**Joshua
3 v 7-13**

*The Israelites
are going to
cross the River
Jordan and
invade Canaan.*

*They've got to
follow behind
the ark of
the covenant,
to show
that they're
following God.*

God's in charge!

It must have been scary for the
Israelites, knowing they would soon
have to fight loads of big armies.

Read Joshua 3 v 7-8

God let them know that He was
supporting Joshua as their leader,
just as He had with Moses. Joshua
would be a great leader.

Read verses 9-10

Uh-oh, the Israelites have to bash
loads of armies before they can live
in the land God promised them.

Unjumble the army anagrams.

A_____
ROSATIME

P_____
ZITZIPEERS

H_____
THESITTI

J_____
IJETBUSES

C_____
ACANINESAT

H_____
IVETHIS

G_____
SHIRTGAGESI

Read verses 11-13

God was going to do an amazing
miracle. He would stop the raging
river Jordan from flowing!

Why?

To show that the

_____ _____

V I L N I G   O D G

was with them (v10)

Wow!

If God can do miracles like that, He
can do ANYTHING for His people!

WEIRD WORDS

Exalt
Put in a high
position, gaining
people's respect

Pray!

Our God is God of the whole
earth (v11, 13)! Nothing is too
hard for Him! Will you turn to
God now with whatever's on your
mind! He can help you!

11

The Israelites have got to cross the rushing River Jordan.

God will lead them from the front...

WEIRD WORDS

Vicinity
Local area

Waders of the ark

Do you remember what was being carried in front of them?

The ark was a special box which Moses had made.

It contained the stones with the 10 Commandments written on them.

When the Israelites saw the ark, it reminded them that God Himself was with them – and that He would keep the promises He had made.

Use the word pool to show how the ark helped them see that God was with them.

way   lead

follow   safe

1. The ark would _____ them into the promised land.

2. They were to keep their eyes on the ark and _____ it.

3. The ark went first, to make a _____ for them to cross.

4. When they did cross, the ark stood still on the river bed until they were all _____ (v17).

Now read Joshua 3 v 14-17

The people followed the ark safely to the other side. This is a great example of how God **saves and protects** His people.

How does God save and protect His people today? Use the same words to fill in the gaps.

1. Jesus is the only one who can _____ us to eternal life.

2. We are to keep our eyes on Jesus and _____ Him.

3. Jesus has made a _____ for us to be forgiven by God, by dying in our place.

4. Jesus will bring His people _____ly home to live with Him forever.

PRAY! Spend time thanking God right now!

Remember remember

**Joshua
4 v 1-24**

An amazing miracle has happened!

God stopped the rushing River Jordan from flowing, to let His people get safely across into the promised land of Canaan!

WEIRD WORDS

Exalted
Put in a high position, gaining people's respect

Revered/stood in awe
Showed great respect

This is something they would remember forever, isn't it? But in the past, the Israelites hadn't been very good at remembering God's miracles. In fact, they often **forgot** the amazing things God had done for them. So this time God gave them something special to do to remind them.

Read Joshua 4 v 1-20

Fill in the missing words from the story. Use the wordsearch and verses 1-20 to help you.

```
O A U H S O J T S M C T
H F R S T T W M R L R U
C S T O N E L O R I G L
I H C H L L C S B G I U
R O I V S R B E D O L F
E N E D A E Q S T D G R
J O R E J N A T F Y A E
Z U F M E M O R I A L W
L R N A D R O J T J K O
F C H I L D R E N H W P
```

Joshua was to choose t_____ men, one from each t_____ (v2). They each took a s_____ from the J_____ (v3) to make a m_____ (v7) for the Israelites and their c_____ (v6).

Joshua built this monument in G_____, close to J_____ (v19). From now on, J_____ was respected, just as M_____ had been (v14).

Building a stone monument sounds a strange thing to do. What's the reason behind it?

Read verses 21-24

It was to remind them of the amazing things G_____ had done for them (v23). Everyone would see that God is p_____ (v24). Everyone would f_____ (respect and obey) the Lord (v24).

Think!
On scrap paper, write down what amazing things God has done for you. (Romans 5 v 8 may help you.)

Action!

Write, draw or make something with the words of Romans 5 v 8 on it. Then you'll have something to remind you of the amazing things God has done.

Luke: Life with Jesus

**Luke
3 v 1-6**

Today we're jumping back into Luke's Gospel.

Remember Elizabeth and Zechariah's son John? God had said he would have a special job to do. Now he's all grown up — so let's find out if he's doing it...

WEIRD WORDS

Tiberius Caesar
Roman Emperor

**Governor/
tetrarch**
Local ruler

The Jordan
Main river in Israel

Salvation
Rescue

Read Luke 3 v 1-3

Luke sets the scene by telling us about some of the local rulers and high priests. The fact that these guys were in charge tells us that the date was about 26AD.

*Luke also reintroduces us to **John the Baptist**. What was John telling people about (v3)? Fill in the vowels (aeiou) to find out.*

1. R__p__nt__nc__

That's turning away from your sinful ways and living God's way instead.

2. B__pt__sm

Being washed in water to show that you've repented and are now living for God.

If you're wondering about getting baptised, ask an older Christian about it.

3. F__rg__v__n__ss of s__ns

People who turn away from sin and turn to God have their sins forgiven by Him.

John was an amazing speaker, telling people to get back to living God's way. *But where did His message come from (v2)?*

It was the W__rd of G__d

It wasn't John's own message. It was God's! 700 years earlier, the prophet Isaiah had predicted that John would have a really important task to do.

Read verses 4-6

Find John's big task in verse 4.

Prepare the way for
the L__rd

Wow!

John was making the way ready for Jesus Christ. Jesus was coming to save people from the punishment for sin. And not just save people in 26AD. The message of Jesus is for ALL PEOPLE (v6)!

That means us too! We all have to decide whether to accept or reject Jesus.

Pray!

As we learn about Jesus in Luke's book, ask God to help you understand why Jesus came to earth.

30

Finding fruit

**Luke
3 v 7-14**

John the Baptist is preparing the way for Jesus by telling people to repent — to turn their backs on sin.

Many people thought that being Jewish (descended from Abraham) was enough to make them right with God. But John had news for them...

Read Luke 3 v 7-8

Their sins wouldn't be forgiven just because they were related to Abraham. They had to turn their backs on sin and trust in **Jesus**.

> So how do we know if someone really has turned to God and had their sins forgiven?

Think!

John tells us that God's people live God's way. It's obvious from what they do and say that they've turned their backs on sin and are serious about serving God. Is that true of you?

Read verse 9

This means...

> **Watch out! Soon Jesus will judge the world. People who refuse to live His way will go to hell.**

This is deadly serious stuff. People who don't turn to Jesus for forgiveness will be punished. And people who **have** had their sins forgiven should live God's way. Here are some examples...

Read verses 10-14

Action!

What action do YOU need to take so that you're living God's way? Something you need to do more, or stop doing?

_____

_____

_____

_____

Pray!

Ask God to help you do those things, so that people around you can see that serving God is more important to you than anything else.

Serious stuff!

**Luke
3 v 15-20**

John the Baptist was preparing the way for Jesus

But the people got a bit confused about who John really was..

WEIRD WORDS

Threshing-floor
Where wheat was separated from bad stuff (**chaff**) using a **winnowing fork**

Unquenchable
Can't put it out!

Exhorted
Strongly warned them about God's punishment

Rebuked
Told off

Herod
Local ruler

Read Luke 3 v 15

Unjumble the anagram.

They thought John was the

M_____

s a s M i e h

The **Messiah** (or *Christ*) was the Rescuer who God had promised would come and save His people. The people thought John might be this amazing man, but John put them straight...

Read verses 16-20

John told everyone the Messiah would come soon. He was talking about **Jesus** — God's Son!

What would Jesus do?

1. Baptise people with the

H_____ S_____
l o y H   t r i p S i

Jesus would give His followers His Holy Spirit to help them live for God (v16).

2. Gather the w_____

h a t e w

into His barn (v17)

Everyone who trusts Jesus' death to rescue them will one day be gathered by Jesus to live with Him forever!

3. Burn up the c_____

f a h f c

Those who ignore Jesus and live only for themselves will be thrown into hell forever.

A lot of people don't like this message and choose to ignore it, just as Herod did (v19-20).

Wow!

Don't ignore John's message! Living a good life... going to church... having Christian parents... **isn't good enough!** God's kingdom is only for people who turn their backs on sin and turn to Jesus to rescue them.

Want to know more? For a free fact sheet on *How to become a Christian*, email
discover@thegoodbook.co.uk
or check out
www.thegoodbook.co.uk/contact-us
to find our UK mailing address.

Father and Son

**Luke
3 v 21-38**

*John the Baptist
is getting
people ready
for Jesus, the
great Rescuer.*

*Time for Jesus
to make an
entrance.*

Imagine the scene: John the Baptist at the river Jordan. People are coming to him and being baptised as they admit how sinful their lives have been. They're making a new start, living for God.

Jesus wanted to be baptised too. But why?

Read Luke 3 v 21-22

When Jesus was baptised, something really special happened.

*Fill in the missing **O**s and **E**s.*

H__av__n was __p__n__d
and the H__ly Spirit cam__
d__wn on J__sus like a
d__ve.

A v__ic__ fr__m h__av__n
said: "Y__u are my S__n,
whom I l__v__; with y__u
I am w__ll pl__as__d."

The voice of God the Father, and the coming of the Holy Spirit, show that Jesus was **God's Son**. He didn't need to repent because God was pleased with Him.

> So why did Jesus line up with loads of sinners to get baptised?

Because Jesus came to **take the place of sinners**. At the beginning of His ministry, Jesus was treated just like a sinner. At the end too, when He died on a cross, Jesus would be treated just like a sinner.

Wow!

God loved Jesus very much. Yet He would punish Jesus on the cross for sins like ours. That shows how much God loves us too.

(Verses 23-38 tell us all about the family Jesus came from. Check it out if you fancy some extra reading.)

Pray!

Spend time thanking God for sending His Son Jesus to us!

WEIRD WORDS

Ministry
Three years of Jesus' life when He taught God's Word

Speak of the devil

Luke
4 v 1-4

Yesterday we discovered that Jesus is God's Son, and that God is very pleased with Him.

Today, Jesus meets the devil.

Read Luke 4 v 1-3

Jesus was in the desert for 40 days without any food. How did He feel?

[ ]

Remember, Jesus was God's Son but He lived on earth as a **human being**, so He got hungry just as we do. He was also tempted by the devil as we are. The devil wanted to destroy Jesus, and now he saw his chance, when Jesus was at His weakest.

What did the devil say (v3)?

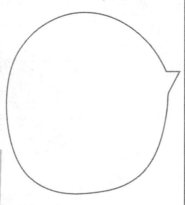

That sounds like a reasonable suggestion, doesn't it? But watch out! **The devil's temptations are never harmless!**

Read verse 4

Jesus quoted part of the Old Testament. Check it out in **Deuteronomy 8 v 3**. It's part of what Moses said to the Israelites.

Complete Moses' words...

Man does not _____

_____

_____

_____

Wow!

If Jesus had listened to the devil and failed to trust God, He'd have been sinful just like us. But Jesus relied on His Father God and nothing else! We too can learn from God's words in the Bible. And we can rely on God for everything we need.

Pray!

1. Ask God to help you fight the devil's temptations.
2. Ask God to help you learn more from His Word, the Bible.
3. Thank God that you can rely on Him for everything you need.

On top of the world?

**Luke
4 v 5-8**

Would you like to be super-powerful?

Want to rule the world?

Yes/No _____

WEIRD WORDS

Authority
Power, ruling over many kingdoms

Splendour
Brilliance, impressiveness

Read Luke 4 v 5-7

The devil is still trying to tempt Jesus to do wrong. Ruling the world sounds tempting, doesn't it? Let's see how Jesus answered the devil.

Read verse 8

Go back one letter (B=A, C=B etc) to reveal Jesus' answer.

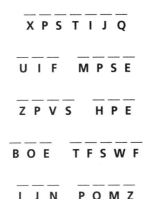

X	P	S	T	I	J	Q

U I F   M P S E

Z P V S   H P E

B O E   T F S W F

I J N   P O M Z

Wow!

We should live for God only. Only He created us. Only He can forgive our wrongs. He deserves to be put first in our lives. Nothing else should become more important to us than God.

What three words did Jesus use in all of His replies to the devil (verses 4, 8, 10)?

Jesus answered the devil's temptations with words from the Bible. Knowing more of the Bible can help us to fight temptation!

Action!

The Bible book *Proverbs* has loads of great verses to memorise and help us throughout our lives. Look at Proverbs chapter 15 and pick a verse to learn. Write it out...

_____

_____

_____

_____

Try to memorise it!

Pray!

Ask God to help you worship Him and nothing else. Thank God for giving us the Bible so that we have His words to help us fight sin and temptation.

Tried and tested

**Luke
4 v 9-13**

*The devil is trying
to tempt Jesus to
do wrong.*

*But he's failed
with his first two
attempts, so he
changes tactics.*

Read Luke 4 v 9-11

That seems an unlikely way of trapping Jesus. But the devil was craftily using part of the Bible to trick Jesus (Psalm 91 v 11-12).

The Problem

If the devil was quoting the Bible, then surely God's angels **would** have rescued Jesus.

The Answer

But the devil was **twisting** God's Word to try to tempt Jesus to do wrong. God's promise is to look after us when we are living His way. Not when we go our own way. Like jumping off the top of buildings just to test Him!

Read verse 12

Jesus wouldn't listen to the devil's twisting of God's Word. Jesus quoted a part of the Bible that says we shouldn't put God to the test. Jesus would have been **testing** God's care of Him if He had jumped.

Wow!

We shouldn't test God's care for us by doing unnecessary, dangerous things and expecting Him to keep us safe!

Read verse 13

The devil was beaten!

Think!

Write down some of the things you're tempted to do which you know are wrong.

_____

_____

_____

_____

_____

_____

Pray!

Now ask God to help you fight those temptations. It might take you a long time, but God can help you turn your back on those things and live His way more and more.

Can you remember the proverb you learned yesterday? If not, try memorising it again.

Read all about it!

Jesus had been in the desert for 40 days, without food, but He stood up to the devil's temptations. Next, Jesus returned to Nazareth, the area where He'd grown up.

Read Luke 4 v 14-21

Jesus was asked to read part of Isaiah, a book in the Old Testament. The bit Jesus read was all about Himself!

Verse 18 tells us four things that Jesus came to do. Fill in the missing letters please.

1. Proclaim g__ __d ne__s to the __oor

Here, the poor means people who realise they have disobeyed God and need to turn from their sinful ways. The **good news** is that Jesus came to rescue people from the punishment for their sin. They can be forgiven!

2. Freed__m for __risoners

People are **trapped** by sin. Sin is in charge of their lives. They live for themselves instead of for God. But Jesus wants to set people **free** from sin.

3. Give r__c__very of __ight to the b__ind

People are **blinded** by their sin. They live only for themselves. They can't see that they should be living for God.

4. Rele__se the opp__ess__d

People may be trapped by their sin, but Jesus wants to **release** them. He died on the cross and was raised back to life to beat sin once and for all. If we turn to Jesus and ask for forgiveness, He will set us free from all our wrongs!

Pray!

Read through what Jesus came to do, then spend time thanking Him!

For the free e-booklet *Why did Jesus come?* email discover@thegoodbook.co.uk or check out www.thegoodbook.co.uk/contact-us to find our UK mailing address.

37

Luke 4 v 22-30

Jesus was saying amazing things.

How would the people react?

WEIRD WORDS

Gracious words
Talking about God's goodness

Proverb
Wise saying

Physician
Doctor

Capernaum
City where Jesus preached and did many miracles

Sky was shut
It didn't rain!

Leprosy
Skin disease

Cleansed
Healed of leprosy

Doctor who?

Read Luke 4 v 22-24

The people wanted Him to perform miracles and healings. But Jesus came to do so much more.

Read verses 25-27

The people were suddenly offended. Jesus was saying...

> **I've not come to save just you Israelites. I will save people from other nations too, when you reject me.**

Wow!

Jesus didn't only come to rescue God's chosen people, the Israelites. ANYONE can trust Jesus to rescue them from sin! That's great news for us. But these people didn't think so...

Read verses 28-30

They tried to kill Him! But Jesus is God's Son, so He just walked straight past them.

Even in His home town, people were against Jesus. And today people often don't want to hear about Jesus.

Circle the words that describe a wrong reaction to Jesus' message.

RUDE   INTERESTED

ACCEPTING   TEASING

BELIEVING   EMBARRASSED

CRUEL   LISTENING

*From the circled words, rearrange the **BOLD** letters to describe Christians who get hassled for telling people about Jesus.*

B__ __ __ __ __ __

People were furious when Jesus told them the truth. And we can expect hassle when we tell people the truth about Jesus. But God is pleased when we have the courage to tell people about Him.

Pray!

Thank God that ANYONE can be rescued by Jesus. Ask Him to help you tell your friends this great truth.

Answer: BLESSED — That's what Matthew 5 v 11-12 is all about.

38

Luke 4 v 31-37

We're reading Luke's book about Jesus.

Luke has already given us lots of evidence that Jesus is God's Son.

Today he gives us some more.

WEIRD WORDS

Sabbath
Jewish rest day

Demons/ impure spirits
Evil spirits that live in people, causing them to sin or be ill

Holy One of God
Jesus was perfect and was sent by God

Sternly
Very seriously

Spirit-splatting stuff

Read Luke 4 v 31-32

*To find the first piece of evidence about Jesus, take **every 3rd letter** starting with the first **J**.*

J T A E H U S E T U S H S P O
T I R A R I U I T G T Y H K O T
N V W E E I W R T W E H H V
A O I U J L T E S H S P O U I R
S R I W I T A T Y S S

1. J_____

_____ _____

The people couldn't believe their ears! Jesus' teaching didn't come from other people. His teaching came **straight from God**, His Father.

Wow!

We're so privileged. We get to read the words of Jesus Christ! We get teaching straight from God's Son!

So keep listening to what He says in Luke's book.

Read verses 33-34

Evil/impure spirits are God's enemies and they often made people very ill. But God is far more powerful than any evil spirit!

*Now write down every 3rd letter beginning with the **T**.*

2. T_____

_____

The evil spirit called Jesus **the Holy One of God**. It knew that Jesus had been sent by God, so it was terrified.

Read verses 35-37

*Now write down every 3rd letter, beginning with the **A**.*

3. A_____

_____

Jesus commanded the spirit to leave the man, and it did! Jesus was **in charge**. Nothing is more powerful than Jesus.

Are **you** as amazed by Jesus as these people were (v36)?

Pray!

Thank Jesus that we can read His amazing teaching.
And thank Him that nothing is more powerful than Him.

Fever pitch

**Luke
4 v 38-44**

So far we've found out that Jesus is God's Son.

He's an awesome teacher who has power over evil spirits. And that's not all...

WEIRD WORDS

Simon
The disciple also known as Peter or Simon Peter

Rebuked
Told off

The Messiah
The King who would rescue God's people

Solitary
Lonely

Read Luke 4 v 38-39

Simon's mother-in-law was ill.

Fill in the missing Es to show what happened when Jesus went to see her.

**The f__v__r l__ft h__r. Sh__
got up and b__gan to wait
on th__m.**

That's incredible! Jesus healed her instantly. No one but Jesus could heal someone that quickly. In a second she was well enough to get a meal for Him and His disciples.

Read verses 40-41

Fill in the missing As and Ss.

**Je__u__ he__led
people who had v__riou__
kinds of __ickness. He
also drove out demon__
from m__ny people.**

**JESUS HAS COMPLETE
POWER OVER ILLNESS!**

Pray!

Do you know anyone who is ill?

_____

It's not always part of God's plan for people to get better immediately. But we can ask God to heal them because He has the power to do it! So why not pray for them now?!

Read Luke 42-44

Why did Jesus want to leave the town? Fill in the missing Es & Os.

**To pr__claim the
g__ __d n__ws of the
kingd__m of G__d**

It was Jesus' mission to tell people to turn away from sin and start living God's way.

Wow!

That's the mission of all Christians. To spread the good news that everyone can be a part of God's kingdom — no longer living for themselves but living with God as King of their lives.

Pray!

Who do you want to tell about God's kingdom?

_____

_____

Ask God to give you the chance to tell them about how Jesus can turn their lives around.

Simple for Simon

**Luke
5 v 1-11**

*Fishermen are
tough lads.*

*They have
a very hard,
physical job.*

*And they smell
a bit, er, fishy
too.*

*Not really the
kind of people
you'd expect
Jesus to hang
out with.*

WEIRD WORDS

Sinful
Disobedient to God

Read Luke 5 v 1-5

After a hard night's work, these
fishermen had not caught a single
fish! But Jesus was about to change
that. And He was going to change
their lives too.

> **Try fishing again in
> deeper water.**

It was a strange suggestion.

Especially as fish in deep sea are
normally caught at night. Simon
must have been baffled.

> **That doesn't make any
> sense. But, because
> you say so, I'll let
> down the nets.**

Read verses 6-7

That's an incredible result! Jesus
did this miracle to prove to the
fishermen that He was God's
Son. Next, He would change their
whole lives...

Read verses 8-11

*Cross out the Js, Xs and Zs to reveal
what Simon Peter said.*

ZXJGOXAJWAXXJYZ
FXRJOJJMZXMXEJZJLXO
ZRXDXZIJXXAMZZXAJSZ
IXNFJZJXUXLZZMJAZNJ

G_____

_____

_____

Simon Peter thought he was far
too sinful to be anywhere near
Jesus. But Jesus wants people like
Simon Peter to follow Him. Jesus
wants people to turn away from
their sinful ways and start living His
way. And that's exactly what these
fishermen did!

What else did Jesus say (v10)?

> **From now on you will**
>
> _____

Wow!

That doesn't mean catching people
in large nets. It means telling
people about Jesus, so they can
follow Him too.

Pray!

Thank Jesus that He wants sinful
people like us to follow Him!
Thank Him that He wants YOU to
catch other people for Him.

**Luke
5 v 12-26**

Dropping in

Read Luke 5 v 12-16

If you had the skin disease leprosy, no one would come near you. But Jesus touched this man and healed him. He showed love for a man who no one would go near.

Read verses 17-20

These men were so desperate for Jesus to heal their friend that they let him down through a hole in the roof!

What did Jesus say to the man (v20)?

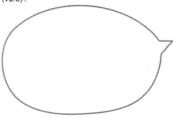

If the man needed to **walk**, why did Jesus talk to him about **sin**?

Wow!

Sin is more than just doing wrong stuff. Sin is doing what **we** want instead of what **God** wants. Sin separates us from God. This man couldn't walk, but he had a far bigger problem: SIN.

Jesus claimed to have the power to forgive sins! This upset some of the religious leaders...

Read verse 21

They couldn't believe that Jesus was claiming to have the same power as God. But Jesus **is** God, so He proved it to them.

Read verses 22-26

Which of these is easiest to say?

A	B
Your sins are forgiven	Get up and walk

It's easier to say **A** because no one can see if it's true or not! So, to show that He really does have power to forgive sins, Jesus also said **B**! And then He healed the man in front of everyone!

Jesus proved that He has the power to forgive sins.

Think!

Only Jesus has the power to forgive sins. Have you asked Him to forgive yours?
If you want to, tell Him you're SORRY for letting Him down. And that you want to live for Him, not yourself. Ask Him to FORGIVE you. Make sure you tell an older Christian you've asked Jesus to forgive you.

42

**Luke
5 v 27-32**

*Which of these
needs a doctor?*

Rob
has a fever and
can barely move

Grace
is covered in
green boils!

Jess
feels really,
really healthy

WEIRD WORDS

Sect
Particular group of
Jewish people

Righteous
People who think
they're right with
God

Repentance
Turning away from
sin

Doctor doctor...

*Go back one letter to reveal a
famous phrase.*

_ _   _ _
J U   J T

_ _ _   _ _ _
O P U   U I F

_ _ _ _ _ _ _
I F B M U I Z

_ _ _   _ _ _ _   _
X I P   O F F E   B

_ _ _ _ _ _   _ _ _
E P D U P S   C V U

_ _ _   _ _ _
U I F   J M M

Sounds obvious? Well it wasn't to
the religious leaders.

Read Luke 5 v 27-30

Who did Jesus call to follow Him?

_ _ _ _
M F W J

Levi was also known as **Matthew**
(yep, the disciple who wrote the
Bible book "Matthew"). He was a
tax collector who worked for the
hated Romans.

The Pharisees were horrified
that Jesus made friends with tax
collectors and other people they
didn't respect. They thought He
should only hang out with "good"
people (like them!).

But what's that got to do with **ill
people** and **doctors**?

Read verses 31-32

_ _ _ _ _ _ _ _   means
I F B M U I Z

**people who think
they're good.**

_ _ _
J M M

**means people who know
that they're sinful.**

_ _ _ _ _ _
E P D U P S

That's Jesus — the sin doctor!

Jesus knows that people who think
they're good enough won't ask Him
(the sin doctor) to forgive them. But
people who realise how sinful they
are will turn to Jesus for forgiveness.
And He'll **cure** their sin problem!

Pray!

We're all sinners. But not
everyone thinks they need Jesus
to forgive them. How about you?
Talk to God about your answer.

43 Fast and furious

Luke
5 v 33-39

Ever been to a wedding?

Imagine if there were no food, not even a wedding cake!

WEIRD WORDS

Disciples
People who learned from someone

Parable
Story told by Jesus to explain a big truth

Garment
Piece of clothing

Wineskins
Wine bottle made from the skins of an animal

Read Luke 5 v 33-34

The Pharisees and the followers of John the Baptist were **fasting**.

> **FASTING** (going without food for a while) was a sign of being sad. Many Jews fasted twice a week! Either to please God or impress other people.

But there was **no reason** why Jesus' disciples should fast. Jesus compared Himself to a **bridegroom** (v34). His disciples were like wedding guests. They were so happy to be with Jesus (the bridegroom). Why should they be sad and go without food?!

Read verse 35

Jesus knew that He would soon **die**. When that happened, His followers would be really sad. Then they'd fast. (Yet their sorrow wouldn't last for long — God would raise Jesus back to life!)

The message about Jesus is that He came to RESCUE us. He died in our place, so that we can be friends with God.

But the Pharisees said that people had to keep a set of rules to be friends with God.

The two messages don't mix!

Read verses 36-39

… and draw what's missing in the boxes.

You wouldn't sew a new

onto an old

or pour new

into old

- If you patch up **old** clothes with **new** material, they'll rip!

- If you pour **new** wine into brittle **old** wineskins, they'll split.

If you try to fit the message of **Jesus** into a human set of rules, it won't work. The **Pharisees** said: *"You must keep our rules to please God".* **Jesus** said: *"Repent (turn away from your sin) and believe the good news".*

You can't become a Christian by keeping rules or trying to be good. Only by **trusting Jesus** to forgive your sin.

Pray!

Thank God that you don't need to keep a set of rules to be His friend. Thank Him for sending Jesus as your Rescuer.

Romans: Right with God

**Romans
5 v 1**

Last issue, we started reading the book of Romans.

It's a letter Paul wrote to Christians in Rome, Italy.

It's all about how we can become RIGHT WITH GOD.

Read Romans 5 v 1. Twice!

What's that all about?!

Justified
To be put right with God, having all your sins forgiven. It's **just as if I'd** never sinned.

Faith
Trusting in Jesus' death on the cross to put us right with God.

*So how does this **justified through faith** thing work? Check out the explanations below. Fill in the gaps using the word pool.*

> deserve   died   faith
> forgiven   Jesus   peace
> punishes   sinning   trusts

PROBLEM
God rightly p_____ people for s_____ against Him. Fortunately for us, He has also made a way for us to escape our punishment!

SOLUTION
Jesus d_____ on the cross to take the punishment we d_____ for sinning! Anyone who t_____ in Jesus' death in their place can be f_____!

RESULT
J_____ has taken the punishment. So everyone who has f_____ in Jesus is now at p_____ with God!

How cool is that?!

Still puzzled? Well, think of an **umbrella**. It gets wet so that we can stay dry. It comes between us and the rain.

Jesus comes between us and God's punishment so that we can be at peace with God.

Think!
But it's not automatic. God's peace is available to anyone, but you have to put your faith in Jesus to forgive you. Have you done that yet?

Pray!

Thank God that Jesus has done everything we need to be at peace with God.

Glory days

**Romans
5 v 1-5**

*What are
Christians like?*

really boring ☐

incredibly cool ☐

pretty average ☐

WEIRD WORDS

Justified
Right with God

Grace
God giving us far
more than we
deserve

Perseverance
Sticking at living for
God

Holy Spirit
We'll learn about
the Holy Spirit
tomorrow!

Christians can be any of those
things! Christians come in all
shapes and sizes. Some seem pretty
normal, some are cool and yes,
some are incredibly booooring!
But all Christians share something
amazing...

Read Romans 5 v 1-5

Having faith in Jesus is like being
allowed into God's treasure
rooms. That's what **grace** means
— God giving us gifts that we
don't deserve.

*Fill in the columns in the bottom
grid in the right order to reveal one
of the great gifts that God gives to
Christians (v2).*

3	7	5	4	9	1	8	2	6
D		W			A		N	E
B	T	A	O					S
		H	T		I		N	E
O	O	E	P			F	H	
E	O	G		Y	T	R	H	L
F	D	G					O	O

1	2	3	4	5	6	7	8	9
	N							
	N							
	H						F	
	H						R	
	O							

**We get to share God's
GLORY! We've got eternal
life to look forward to!**

Sometimes we hope for things and
are disappointed. A Christian's hope
isn't like that. *What does **verse 5**
tell us about our hope of eternal life
with God?*

This hope does not

_____

Have you ever been waiting for your
friends to arrive for your birthday
party, nervously hoping that
everyone turns up? Because it would
be embarrassing if they didn't!

A Christian's hope isn't like that.
We know for **sure** that we will get
eternal life. That's why Paul says we
won't be put to shame.

*Because our hope's certain, what
can we do (v2)?*

_____ **in the hope of
the glory of God.**

Normally we think of boasting
as a bad thing (and it is, if we're
boasting about ourselves!). But we
should be so **happy** and **excited**
about what **Jesus** has done to give
us eternal life that we want to tell
everyone about it!

Wow!

Christians can be joyful, whatever
happens to them, because their
hope of eternal life is CERTAIN.
Do you want to thank God now?!

Lots of love

**Romans
5 v 5-8**

So far, Paul has told us how Jesus can make people right with God.

He's also told us about two great gifts that God gives to His people: joy and peace.

Time for great gift number three...

WEIRD WORDS

Christ
The King who came to rescue God's people

Ungodly
Sinful

Righteous
Good and godly

Read Romans 5 v 5 and 8

… and see if you can work out what great gift number three is.

 L _ _ _

We all want to be loved.

And God's love is the best there is! Verse 5 says that God has **poured out** His love into Christians' hearts!

Holy Spirit

The Holy Spirit is God. Every Christian has the Holy Spirit in them all the time, helping them to live for God. The Holy Spirit fills believers with God's love.

> But what about the times when we just don't feel as if God loves us?

God has given us undeniable proof of His amazing love!

Read about it in verses 6-8

Sometimes we see headlines like the one on that newspaper. Love can lead someone to give up their own life for their friends or family. But **God's love** is even greater than that!

Fill in the blanks using the word blocks.

died for	hate
reject	loves

Sinners like us

h_____ Jesus, and we

_____ Him.

Jesus l_____ sinners

like us. So He

_____ us!

Wow!

Christians know that God loves them because He sent His Son Jesus to die for them. Even though they disobeyed and hated Him.

Pray!

Thank God for His awesome love. Ask Him to keep reminding you of how much He loves you.

47

**Romans
5 v 9-11**

*We're reading
Paul's letter to
the Christians in
Rome.*

*He's telling us
about the great
things Jesus has
done for us.*

Unstoppable love!

> I used to feel sure that
> Jesus loved me, but now I
> just don't know.

Do you ever feel like this?
It's understandable if you do (so
don't worry about it!). But there's
no need to feel that way.

Yesterday we found out that
Christians can be **certain** of God's
love. If we remember that, it will
help us with our doubts.

Read Romans 5 v 9-10

Wow! That's awesome stuff! Read
the verses again, using the **weird
word** box.

Here's what Paul says is true for
every Christian:

```
┌──────────┐
│ Once I   │
│ was...   │
└──────────┘
     ↓
┌────────────────────────┐
│     GOD'S ENEMY        │
└────────────────────────┘
     ↓                ↓
┌──────────┐   ┌──────────────┐
│ Now      │   │ Jesus died   │
│ I am...  │   │ to make me   │
└──────────┘   └──────────────┘
     ↓                ↓
┌────────────────────────┐
│     GOD'S FRIEND       │
└────────────────────────┘
     ↓                ↓
┌──────────┐   ┌──────────────┐
│ I always │   │ Jesus lives  │
│ will be..│   │ to keep me   │
└──────────┘   └──────────────┘
     ↓                ↓
┌────────────────────────┐
│     GOD'S FRIEND       │
└────────────────────────┘
```

Jesus loved you (His sinful enemy)
enough to die for you.

So He'll definitely carry on loving
you now he has made you His
friend!

Action!

Paul was absolutely certain that
NOTHING could separate Christians
from God's love.

Find **Romans 8 v 38-39** and write it
out or turn it into a poster.

If you're a Christian, that's true for
you! So you've got loads to be really
happy about!

Read Romans 5 v 11

Pray!

Will you "boast" (tell others)
about what God has done? Spend
time thanking Him for sending His
Son Jesus to die for YOU.

WEIRD WORDS

**Justified by His
blood**
Jesus died on
the cross so that
people can be
right with God

God's wrath
God's anger
because of our sin
against Him

Reconciled
A damaged
relationship
put right

48

**Romans
5 v 12-14**

*Grilled
grasshopper!
Marmite
sandwiches!
Babies' nappies!*

*What's the
most disgusting
thing you can
think of?*

_____

_____

_____

WEIRD WORDS

Sin
Disobeying God.
Doing what we
want instead of
what God wants.

The law
The way God wants
us to live

Reigned
Ruled

Sin disease

Sin is far more disgusting!!!

Read Romans 5 v 12-14

Sin came to the world through Adam

So everyone in the world is sinful

Sin results in death for everyone

> That seems a bit unfair. One person disobeys and we're all punished!

Sin is like a disease. One person was the first to catch it, and it spread around as people came into contact with it. Sin entered the world through one man, but we've all caught the sin disease by disobeying God.

When Adam fell into sin, we all fell with him. But there's no point blaming him and thinking we could have done any better.

Every one of us has **chosen** to sin. We've chosen to live for ourselves instead of living for God.

Adam, the first man, sinned for all of us. But we've all sinned too.

Adam brought death into the world. But we all deserve death because we are all sinners.

Wow!

We have all sinned, and the punishment for our sin is death. Tomorrow Paul tells us how we can be cured!

Pray!

Ask God for your friends to realise how sinful they are and that they need to say sorry to God. Write down their names if you like:

_____

_____

Extra: verse 13 is about God's Law. We'll find out more about that tomorrow.

Amazing grace!

49

**Romans
5 v 15-21**

Adam

Yesterday we discovered how Adam sinned and brought God's punishment into the world.

WEIRD WORDS

Trespass
Sin

Condemnation
Punishment in hell

Justification
Forgiveness

Abundant provision
Lots of it!

Righteousness
Being right with God

The law
How God wants us to live

Adam's sin had **disastrous** results for everyone. But what Jesus did has wonderful results.

Read Romans 5 v 15-19

The key phrase in these tricky verses is **"MUCH MORE"**. There's no comparison. What Jesus did is **much more** amazing than what Adam did!

Fill in the missing words to compare Jesus with Adam.

Adam

1. One m_____ (v15)

2.Committed o_____ sin(v16)

3. A_____ people are condemned as sinners (v18)

4. Death for sinners (v21)

All of us must suffer these terrible results, unless we're rescued. All of us must die because all of us have Adam's sin. **That includes you!**

Jesus

1. O_____ man (v15)

2. On the cross, He dealt with m_____ sins (v16)

3. Many people made r_____ with God (v19)

4. Eternal l_____ for believers (v21)

Only some people will have eternal life because only some people trust in Jesus. **Does that include you?**

Read verses 20-21

God's law (in the Bible) shows us how we should live for Him.

It also shows us how we fail to do this and keep disobeying Him. So now we know that we're sinners, we're more likely to ask Jesus to forgive us. God's **grace** is at work!

Grace
We've let God down many times and deserve His punishment. **But** instead, God offers us the undeserved gift of forgiveness through Jesus' death for us.

That's what **GRACE** is.

When **sin** is in charge of our lives the result is **death**. When **God** is in charge of our lives the result is **eternal life** (v21).

What rules **your** life?

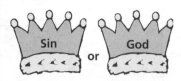

Pray!

Thank God that Jesus beat sin for people like you and me.
If sin is in charge of your life, will you say sorry to God and ask Him to forgive you and take charge of your life?

**Romans
6 v 1-7**

*Time to remind
ourselves of
some tricky
words...*

WEIRD WORDS

Grace
God giving us far
more than we
deserve

Sin
Disobeying God

Baptism
Being dunked
under water to
show that God
has washed away
your wrongs.
When Romans was
written, people
were baptised
as soon as they
became Christians.

Dead and buried

Read Romans 6 v 1-4
What's all that about then?

> **Jesus died on the cross
> to take the punishment
> we deserve. He died for
> our sin!**

> **So when you become a
> Christian you have all
> your wrongs FORGIVEN
> by Jesus.**

> **It is as though your
> sinful life has DIED
> with Jesus.**

> **You no longer want to
> disobey God. You want
> to please Him!**

Take another peek at **verses 1-2**.
We shouldn't keep on doing wrong
now we've turned our backs on sin!

OK, so we won't beat sin every time
and will still mess up. But we should
try not to do those things that we
know displease God. If we mess up,

we should say sorry to God. And try
to do better next time.

Think!
What wrong things do you find it
hard to stop doing?

_____

_____

_____

Read verses 5-7

Resurrection
That means being raised from
death to new life. Three days
after Jesus was crucified, God
resurrected Him from the dead, and
He never died again!

Verses 5-7 are about people who
have trusted Jesus to forgive their
wrongs — Christians. They have
shared in Jesus' death. Their old
sinful way of living **died** when
Jesus died!

Pray!

Say sorry to God for the stuff
you wrote down under Think!
Ask Him to help you cut those
things out of your life. And thank
God for sending Jesus to die in
our place.

Alive and kicking!

**Romans
6 v 8-14**

**Jesus died
for our sin.**

**When you
become a
Christian,
your sinful
life has died
with Jesus!**

**You no
longer want
to disobey
God. You
want to
please Him!**

WEIRD WORDS

Mastery
Control

**Reign in your
mortal body**
Rule your life

**Instrument of
righteousness**
A thing to serve
God with!

Read Romans 6 v 8-11

Christians share in Jesus Christ's **death** and they also share His risen **life**! They are dead to sin — it no longer rules them!

To God it's as if they have become fully alive for the first time. Christians can now live **God's way** rather than sin's way.

Verse 10 calls this **living to God** instead of living to sin.

Read verses 12-13

Think of something that can be used for both good and bad purposes. We've filled in one example for you.

**A knife can
chop food
or kill.**

It's the same with us. We can either use our bodies to please God or to offend Him.

In the boxes below, write how these parts of the body can be used to do God's work or to do things that offend God.

WICKEDNESS (used for wrong)	RIGHTEOUSNESS (used for good)

Read verse 14

Sin is not our master, so we shouldn't do the stuff in the left hand column. We've been **set free by God's grace** to do the things in the right hand column.

Pray!

Tell God about the times you find it hard to live the way He wants you to. Ask Him to use you to serve Him. Then do something about it!

Saving slaves!

Romans
6 v 15-18

Welcome to the Discover slave market.

In slave markets in Bible times, rich people would decide which slaves to buy, and the slaves had no say in the matter.

Here it's the slaves who choose their masters!

So step right this way. What are YOU going to choose to be a slave to?

SIN OR **OBEDIENCE TO GOD**

Read Romans 6 v 16

Now unjumble the anagrams.

Being a slave to s_____
n i s

leads to d_____. Being
t h a d e

a s_____ to God means
v e a l s

obeying G____ and leads to
o d G

being put r_____ with
t h r i g

God (that's what

righteousness means).

It's your choice...

Slaves to sin
Disobeying God
Living for ourselves
Eternal death in hell

or God's slaves
Obeying God
Living for God
Eternal life in heaven

Think!

Have you chosen yet? Have you turned to God, said sorry for disobeying Him and asked Him to forgive you?

Want to know how to choose to serve God instead of sin? For a free fact sheet on how to become a Christian, email discover@thegoodbook.co.uk or check out www.thegoodbook.co.uk/contact-us to find our UK mailing address.

Read verses 15-18

Before someone becomes a Christian they are a **slave to sin**. But when they trust in Jesus, God makes them **free from sin** and free to serve God.

That doesn't mean we won't still mess up sometimes. But it does mean that we can't do whatever we want. We now **live for God** and that means turning our backs on sinful stuff we used to enjoy.

Pray!

Thank God for being such a good and loving master. Ask Him to help you serve Him. Ask God to help you to see the things in your life you need to change.

53

Romans 6 v 19-23

WEIRD WORDS

Impurity
Sin

Holiness
Set apart for God. Living a life that is pleasing to God.

Pay day

When people look for jobs, two of the things they bear in mind are the **wages** (pay) and other **benefits** offered. These help you to know whether it's the right job for you.

It's important to get the right job, but even more important to live the right kind of life. Over the last few days, we've seen that we all serve one of two masters — God or sin. Let's see how they match up.

Romans 6 v 19-23

> **SLAVE TO SIN**
>
> **Benefit: Freedom from**
> r_____ss (v20)
>
> **Wages: D_____ (v23)**

> **SLAVE TO GOD**
> **Benefit: H_____ss (v22)**
> **Wages: None! But check out the fantastic free gift in v23!**

Read verse 23 again

> The w_____
> of sin is death...

If sin is in charge of our lives, everlasting death is what we deserve.

> ...but the g_____
> of God is eternal life

If God is in charge of our lives, we still deserve death for our sin, but instead we get eternal life as a gift from God.

Birthday presents — we don't earn them. We are given them by people who love us enough to give us nice stuff.

God loves us so much that He gives us what we could never earn for ourselves — **forgiveness and eternal life with Him**.

Pray!

God hasn't left us to the eternal death we deserve. He gives eternal life to anyone who asks Him to set them free from sin. Thank Him! Loads! Keep praying for your friends to turn to God so they receive this great gift too.

54

Joshua: Follow the leader

Joshua
5 v 1-12

Back to the story of Joshua.

God helped the Israelites cross the River Jordan. Now they're in the land God promised them.

Amorite/ Canaanite
The people who lived in Canaan

Flint
Sharp rock

Reproach
Disgrace, shame

Unleavened
Without yeast

Manna
Special bread from God

Read Joshua 5 v 1-3

Confused about circumcision?

All male Israelites had a bit of skin around the penis cut off. Ouch! It was a sign of belonging to God's special people.

So why did these men have to be circumcised?

Read verses 4-8 *and use the word pool to fill in the gaps.*

> Canaan   trust
> desert   disobedient
> circumcised   Moses
> God   punished

When M_____ was leader of the Israelites, the people disobeyed G_____ and refused to enter C_____. God p_____ them, making them wander around the d_____ for 40 years. Once all of the d_____ Israelites had died, their children were able to go into Canaan and start over again. By getting c_____, they were promising to t_____ God and live His way from now on.

Read verses 9-12

Verse 9 means that God took away the shame of having to live in someone else's land. He'd now given them their own land — Canaan — to live in!

They celebrated with a Passover feast to remember God rescuing them from Egypt (it's in Exodus 12).

It reminded them that God had rescued them. And that He'd kept His promise of bringing them into a land with plenty of food to eat (v12).

Think & pray!

We don't have to get circumcised these days! But we do have to show our loyalty to God in the way we live. How can YOU do that? Ask God to help you.

Surround sound

**Joshua
5 v 13 – 6 v 11**

*Joshua and all
the Israelites are
outside the well-
defended city of
Jericho.*

*How will they
ever be able to
conquer it?!*

WEIRD WORDS

Reverence
Great respect

Holy
Special because the
commander of God's
army is there

**Ark of the
covenant**
Large wooden box
which was a sign
that God was there
with His people

Read Joshua 5 v 13-15

That was a shock! Joshua was
visited by the commander of God's
heavenly army! It must have been so
encouraging for the Israelites. They
were not on their own in this battle;
God's army was fighting with them!
God was in control, helping His
people invade Canaan.

Read Joshua 6 v 1-2

> **I'm going to give you
> Jericho — you just need to
> obey my commands.**

That's great news from God!

Read verses 3-5
*Complete God's plan by filling in the
missing numbers.*

**March around the city
_____ a day for
_____ days. Get
_____ priests to carry
trumpets in front of the
ark. On the _____th
day, march around the
city _____ times
with the priests blowing
trumpets. When they blast
out _____ long note, get
all the people to shout. Then
the walls of the city
will fall down!**

What an incredible plan!

Read verses 6-11
Did Joshua and the people start to
obey God's plan?

YES/NO _____

They were up against a city full
of armed soldiers. Marching with
the ark showed that God was
with them. They obeyed God and
followed His plans.

Read what God had said to Joshua
earlier in **Joshua 1 v 9**.

Pray!

Thank God that His people
(Christians) can be strong and
courageous because He is always
with them! And His plans always
work out!

56

**Joshua
6 v 12-21**

Yesterday we found out God's plan for conquering Jericho.

Let's see if it worked...

WEIRD WORDS

Devoted things
The things mentioned in verse 19

Liable to destruction
Deserving God's punishment

Articles
Things

Sacred
Set aside for God

Treasury
Treasure rooms

Wall fall down

Read Joshua 6 v 12-14

What was carried in the middle of the procession?

Priests carried the ark of the Lord to show that **God** was there with them, helping them defeat the enemy.

Read verses 15-21

The people obeyed God's commands and the city walls fell down! God was in charge, giving His people victory!

But the people had to obey another of God's commands.

God had conquered Jericho for His people, and everything in the city had to be devoted (given) to Him. Some of it was kept in a special place. The rest had to be destroyed.

What was to be kept in the Lord's treasure rooms (v19)?

And what had to be destroyed (v21)?

That sounds harsh, but these people had rejected God and disobeyed Him and deserved to be punished.

Wow!

It's a sad truth but everyone who disobeys God and refuses to live His way will be punished. One day, everyone who rejects God will be punished severely by Him.

Pray!

Think of people you know who reject God. Plead with God to rescue them from their sinful ways so that they turn to Him. Maybe you can write their names in a notebook and try to pray for them every day.

**Joshua
6 v 22-27**

Jericho has been destroyed, and all of the people killed.

Well, not quite ALL of them...

Safe or sorry?

Read Joshua 6 v 24, 26 & 27

God punished the people of Jericho for going against Him.

In fact, if anyone tried to rebuild Jericho, they'd be punished too.

And that's what happened 500 years later when a man called Hiel did just that. God kept His promise and punished him (1 Kings 16 v 34).

So Jericho was destroyed, but God saved one family from the city. Any idea whose family it was?

R_____

Flick back to Joshua chapter 2 if you need a reminder. Then fill in the vowels (aeiou) to complete the story.

> J__sh__ __ sent tw__
> sp__ __s to check out
> J__r__ch__. The k__ng of
> J__r__ch__ found out, so
> R__h__b hid the sp__ __s and
> h__lp__d them to escape.
> The spies pr__m__s__d that
> R__h__b and her f__m__ly
> would be kept s__f__.

So would God keep that promise?

Read Joshua 6 v 22-25

Rahab had trusted God and He rescued her!

Think!

Today, people who put their trust in God to save them will be rescued from their sins. Have you trusted God to rescue you?

Pray!

Who do you know who needs rescuing from their sinful ways? (Maybe even yourself.) Ask God to show them that they need Him. Ask Him to rescue them.

Keep praying for the people you prayed for yesterday.
Is there anyone you can add to your prayer list?

WEIRD WORDS

Oath
Promise

Solemn
Very serious

Firstborn son
Eldest son

Achan pain

**Joshua
7 v 1-9**

Remember what God said in **Joshua 6 v 18?**

> **Keep away from the devoted things**

Now read Joshua 7 v 1

Big mistake! A guy called Achan stole some of the things that were devoted to God.

*Cross out all the **X**s, **Y**s and **Z**s to find out what happened.*

**G O X X D Z Y S A N Y X G E R
X B U R N E D Z Y X A G A Z Z
I N S Y X T I S Z R A X Y E L Z Z**

__ __ __ __'
__ __ __ __ __
__ __ __ __ __ __
__ __ __ __ __ __
__ __ __ __ __ __

If one Israelite disobeyed God, then all of the Israelites would be punished. That's how seriously God treats sin and disobeying Him.

Read verses 2-5

The Israelites were confident they could easily conquer the small town of Ai. But God punished the Israelites for disobeying Him, and so the people of Ai surprisingly defeated the Israelites!

WEIRD WORDS

Unfaithful
Disobedient

Devoted things
Treasures that belonged to God

Weary
Tire out

Routed
Totally defeated

Elders
Leaders

**Tore his clothes/
Sprinkled dust on their heads**
Signs of great sadness

Sovereign LORD
God, who is in control of everything

Read verses 6-9

Joshua couldn't work out what had gone wrong...

Had God brought them over the River Jordan just so that their enemies could destroy them?

YES/NO _____

Would it have been better to have stayed on the other side of the Jordan?

YES/NO _____

Would the Canaanites and other nations wipe out Israel's name from the earth?

YES/NO _____

No way! Joshua had got it wrong. God would **never** desert His people. Joshua should have realised that **sin** was the problem. God punished His people. But He would still help them conquer Canaan.

Pray!

Say sorry to God for the times you've blamed Him when things have gone wrong.

59

**Joshua
7 v 10-15**

*God is angry
with His
people, the
Israelites.*

*Time for a
quick recap...*

WEIRD WORDS

**Violated my
covenant**
Broken their
agreement to obey
God

**Liable to
destruction**
Deserving to be
destroyed by God

Consecrate
Wash in a special
way to be clean and
ready for God

Clan
Group of families

Who dunnit?

The Israelites had attacked...

a) Ei   b) Ai   c) O

The army was...

a) defeated   b) victorious

c) eating ham sandwiches

because the Israelites had...

a) forgotten their weapons

b) given up fighting

c) sinned against God

Read Joshua 7 v 10-12

Achan had stolen what should have
been devoted to the Lord. Those
things must now be found and
destroyed! *Rearrange the* **anagrams**
to show what God said:

I _____
    i l w l

_____   _____
  t o n   e b

_____   _____
  t w h i   u y o

**unless you destroy those
things (v12).**

That's a very serious warning.

Think!

God says a similar thing to us:
*Will you keep your sins and be
punished? Or leave your sins and be
one of My people?*

God will not be with us unless we
turn away from our sins.

But how would Joshua find out who
the culprit was?

It's hopeless enough when someone
in your class has stolen something
and no one will own up. The
teacher can't find the culprit in a
class of 30!

Read verses 13-15

There were thousands of Israelites.
Joshua didn't stand a chance of
finding out who had sinned. But
God knew who it was. Tomorrow
we'll see how God punished him.

Bad news!

God treats sin very seriously. He
knows all the wrong things we've
done. We must say sorry and ask
Him to forgive us — or face the
punishment.

Good news!

But there's great news for everyone
who has turned to Jesus and asked
for forgiveness. Their sins have been
wiped away forever! (1 John 1 v 9)

Deadly serious

Joshua
7 v 16-26

Achan

*God is going
to punish the
person who
disobeyed His
commands.*

*It won't be a
pretty sight.*

Here's a list of stuff we shouldn't
do. Mark each one out of 10 for
how serious it is (1 = not serious, 10
= really really bad).

ROTTEN LIST

Stealing   ———
Lying   ———
Disobeying parents   ———
Swearing   ———
Cheating   ———
Jealousy   ———
Bullying   ———
Murder   ———

WEIRD WORDS

Plunder
Things captured
from Jericho

200 shekels
About 2.3kg

50 shekels
About 575g

Coveted
Wanted something
that wasn't his

Valley of Achor
Achor means
trouble

Read Joshua 7 v 16-26

Does that seem unfair to you?

YES/NO _____

But had everyone been warned not
to take any devoted things?
(Joshua 6 v 18)

YES/NO _____

So did Achan deserve the
punishment?

YES/NO _____

The punishment was so extreme
because the crime was so serious.
Disobeying God always is.

Wow!

God hates sin. Really hates it. He
hates it when we disobey Him. Every
sin is serious to God. Every sin is a
grade 10 offence, no matter how
small we think it is.

Sin is so serious that only Jesus
dying on the cross can take away
God's anger and punishment.

Prayer action!

Got anything you want to say
sorry to God about?

_____

_____

_____

_____

Remember, when we say sorry
to God he promises to forgive us
and help us to live his way.

How can you try to avoid doing
these wrong things?

_____

_____

_____

_____

61

Second chance

*The Israelites
had disobeyed
God, so He
let them be
defeated by the
people of Ai.*

They had taken the punishment, so
would they go back to trusting in
God?

Read Joshua 8 v 1-2

The Israelites had disobeyed God
so He punished them. Now they're
back to obeying God and He will
give them victory this time.

*What does God say to them? Cross
out all the Js and Xs, then follow
the maze.*

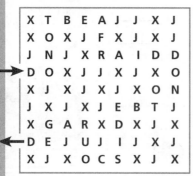

X	T	B	E	A	J	J	X	J
X	O	X	J	F	X	J	X	J
J	N	J	X	R	A	I	D	D
D	O	X	J	J	X	J	X	O
X	J	X	J	X	J	X	O	N
J	X	J	X	J	E	B	T	J
X	G	A	R	X	D	X	J	X
D	E	J	U	J	I	J	X	J
X	J	X	O	C	S	X	J	X

D_____

_____

_____

_____ **(v1)**

Think!

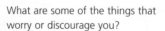

What are some of the things that
worry or discourage you?

_____

_____

_____

Wow!

With God on our side, we don't
need to be afraid or discouraged!
He's in charge and He never lets His
people down. Read **Isaiah 41 v 10**.
How great is that?!

Read verses 3-9

The people would have to fight
hard, but God would give them
victory. He was in control. He
was leading them and they were
following Him.

**Is God in charge of your life?
Do you follow His commands?**

Pray!

Ask God to give you courage to
live for Him and obey Him. And
tell God about the things you
wrote down. Ask Him to comfort
you so that you know He's
looking after you.

WEIRD WORDS

Plunder
Possessions taken
from a defeated
enemy

Livestock
Animals

62

Joshua
8 v 10-23

Oops! This pic
should be of an
AMBUSH, not a
HAM BUSH!

Joshua has
sent a group
of soldiers to
form a secret
ambush.

He commanded
them to lie in
wait around the
far side of the
city of Ai.

WEIRD WORDS

Mustered
Called together

Fugitives
People who are on
the run

Shush! Ambush!

Now it's time for the main Israelite army to march towards Ai ready for the pretend attack.

Read Joshua 8 v 10-23

There were 5 parts to Joshua's plan. In the left-hand circle, number them 1-5 in the order they happened. Then add the verse numbers on the right.

⊙ The soldiers in the ambush raid Ai and set it on fire
v

⊙ The Israelites trap their enemy and defeat them
v

⊙ Joshua and Israelites turn and run for it!
v

⊙ Ai's army marches out to fight Israel
v

⊙ The Israelites approach Ai at night
v

It all went exactly to God's plan. Ai had fallen for the bait and been trapped. With the city blazing, the men of Ai were caught between the two armies of Israel.

Fill the gaps with the words below to discover why the Israelites succeeded this time.

promise   obeyed

God   commands

Because they

_____ God's

_____,

_____ had kept

His _____.

God gave them victory! It was all down to Him.

Think & pray!

What do you think you could do to obey God more?
Be more honest?
Talk to Him more often?
Obey your parents?
Give God more of your time?

_____

_____

_____

_____

_____

Ask God to help you do it!

Over and plunder

The Israelites
had won
a crushing
victory over
the men of Ai.

Now it was
time to finish
off the job.

WEIRD WORDS

Livestock and plunder
Animals and possessions taken from a defeated enemy

Desolate
Ruined and empty

Read Joshua 8 v 23-29

Why did it have to happen that way? Use the code to find out...

1.

The people of Ai were against God, so they deserved His punishment. Years before, God had said He would punish anyone who sinned against Him. Check out **Deuteronomy 9 v 4**.

> Sadly, the same is still true today. People who won't turn to God will be punished by Him.

2.

The Israelites had recently let God down, yet He still gave them gifts! He let the people take animals and possessions from the city (v27).

Pray!

What can you thank God for giving you? Write a list somewhere. Then take some time out to thank Him.

3. It was ____ ____'____

____ ____ ____ ____ ____ ____ ____

The large pile of rocks reminded the people that God had given them the victory (v29). They could not have done it on their own.

> God has won an even greater victory. When Jesus died on the cross and was raised back to life, He won the biggest victory ever! He defeated sin, death and the devil forever! How awesome is that?!

Pray again!

Thank God for sending Jesus to defeat our biggest enemies (sin, death, the devil).

A	B	C	D	E	G	H	I	K	L	N	O	P	R	S	T	U	V	W	Y

Mountain tension

**Joshua
8 v 30-35**

WEIRD WORDS

Altar
Table where gifts (offerings) to God were put

Book of the Law of Moses
First five books of the Bible

Burnt offerings/ Fellowship offerings
Animal meat and fat offered as gifts to God

Foreigners
Non-Israelites, like Rahab

Native-born
Israelites

Levitical priests
Priests from the Israelite tribe of Levi

Read Joshua 8 v 30-35

Thousands and thousands of people gathered to ask God's forgiveness and show their obedience to Him!

Joshua read out all of God's commands for His people.

They would learn exactly how God wanted them to live. God wants **us** to obey His words too.

Think!

Do you need to read more of God's Word (the Bible) and learn more about how God wants you to live?

Look up these great verses from Psalms...
Psalm 78 v 5-7
Psalm 19 v 7-11
Psalm 119 v 11 & 105

Pick a verse, write it out below and try to memorise it.

What did God specifically remind the people of? (v34)

Use yesterday's code to find out.

_ _ _ _ _ _ _ _
_ _ _
_ _ _ _ _ _

If we disobey God and refuse to live His way, His curse will be on us. That means He'll punish us. But if we obey Him, God will stay with us and do amazing things for us! Check out **1 John 3 v 23**.

Action!

We need to keep turning back to God and carry on obeying His Word. On paper, write down some things you can do to make this change. Ask God to help you.

More from Joshua later on...

Luke: Life with Jesus

**Luke
6 v 1-16**

*It's time to get
back to Luke's
book about
Jesus...*

WEIRD WORDS

Sabbath
Jewish rest day

House of God
The temple

Consecrated
Set aside for God

Son of Man
Jesus

Synagogue
Where people met
to learn from God's
Word

**He designated
apostles**
Chose men to send
out and tell people
about Him

Read Luke 6 v 1-5

Jesus' disciples were really hungry so they picked some corn to eat. The Pharisees' rules said this was wrong because it was working on the Sabbath. (Does that sound like work to you?!)

Jesus reminded the Pharisees what King David did when he was starving (it's in **1 Samuel 21 v 1-6**). The Pharisees would have been horrified at that, but God didn't tell David it was wrong. So it can't have been.

Fill in the vowels (aeiou) to reveal what Jesus said (v5).

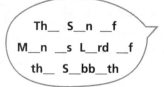

Th__ S__n __f
M__n __s L__rd __f
th__ S__bb__th

Jesus is God, so the Sabbath was His day. And He knew exactly what it was OK to do on God's rest day. In the future, God's people will **rest** forever with Jesus in eternal life.

Read verses 6-11

Jesus healed this man's hand. The Pharisees said this was wrong on a Sabbath. *Complete Jesus' reply (v9).*

Wh__ch is l__wf__l
on the S__bb__th: to do
g__ __d or to do ev__l?
To s__ve l__fe or to
d__str__y it?

Jesus did **good** and healed this man. But the Pharisees were doing **evil** and plotting to harm Jesus (v11).

Action!

Jesus encourages us to do good things for people.

What can you do to help out someone in your family?

_____

_____

_____

Pray!

Ask Jesus to help you serve Him in the way you live. Ask His help to do the good things you wrote down under Action!

(Verses 12-16 tell us about Jesus choosing the twelve apostles.)

Four of the blessed

**Luke
6 v 17-23**

Jesus has just chosen His twelve closest disciples who would travel with Him, learning from Him.

Immediately, they saw Jesus in action...

WEIRD WORDS

Disciples
People taught by Jesus

Exclude you
Leave you out, ignore you

Rejoice
Be really happy

Prophets
God's messengers

Read Luke 6 v 17-19

Jesus is God's Son. He has the power to heal people. Those who came to Him believed that He could heal them. They had faith in Jesus. So they were healed.

Think!

Do you have faith in Jesus? Do you believe He can change your life and the lives of people you know? If so, is your faith in Jesus obvious to others in the way you live?

Read verses 20-23

Blessed means that God is pleased with that person and will give them great things. *Use the **backwards word pool** to find out what kind of person pleases God.*

> deifsitas   etah   hgual
> modgnik   naM   noS
> peew   regnuh   roop
> tlusni

**1. Blessed are the p_____,
for yours is the k_____
of God (v20)**

That means people who realise how sinful they are compared to God's perfection. They get to live with God as King of their lives! And one day, they'll live with Him forever!

**2. Blessed are you who
h_____, for you will be
s_____ (v21)**

That means those who are desperate for God to rescue them from their sin. He will!

**3. Blessed are you who
w_____ now, for you will
l_____ (v21)**

Jesus is talking about those who are upset about sinning against God. He will turn their sadness into happiness.

**4. Blessed are you when
people h_____ you and
i_____ you because of
the S_____ of M_____ (v22)**

Those who get hassled and teased for telling people about Jesus should be happy (v23)! They please God! One day God will reward them.

Pray!

Read through those four things again. Which of those do you need help with?

_____

_____

_____

Turn to God now and ask Him to help you, so that you please Him more.

67

Luke
6 v 24-26

*Yesterday,
Jesus told us
what kind of
people God is
pleased with.*

*Today, He
warns us what
NOT to be like.*

How not to live

Read Luke 6 v 24-26

Woe to you means that God will punish these people for disobeying and rejecting Him. Jesus mentions four kinds of people who displease God. *Unjumble the anagrams to find them.*

1. The r_____ for they
c h i r

have already received their

c_____ (v24)
t o f m o r c

Not just people with stacks of money. It means those who are happy with living for themselves and never give a thought to God. Their happiness will disappear when this life ends and they are separated from God forever.

2. The well f_____ for they
d e f

will go h_____ (v25)
r y h n u g

They think they're OK with God and don't need His help. Too late, they'll realise they needed God to rescue them from their sinful ways.

3. Those who l_____
h u l a g

for they will w_____(v25)
p e w e

People who don't care that they disobey God will weep when they realise that they've chosen to be without Him forever.

4. Those who people
s_____ well of (v26)
a s k e p

People who are popular but don't love God. Their popularity will count for nothing when Jesus returns to judge the world.

Wow!
People who ignore God and live for themselves will one day be punished by Him.

But if you've had your sins forgiven by Jesus, then He has already taken this punishment for you!

Pray!

Think of people you know who refuse to live God's way (maybe yourself). Ask God to turn their lives around, so that they live to please Him!

Love, don't shove!

Luke
6 v 27-36

Imagine what you would do if someone made you look stupid in front of your friends.

Draw a line from the girl to the box that is true for you.

WEIRD WORDS

The Most High
God

Merciful
Showing forgiveness when it's not deserved

> I'd go and punch them on their stupid nose!

> I'd take it, but inside I'd be screaming horrible things at them.

> I'd pray about it and think what I could do for them.

Read Luke 6 v 27-30

We're not only supposed to put up with people who do us wrong. We have to love them and actually do good to them! Don't get revenge, but be forgiving and generous. Pray for the people who hurt you.

Read verse 31

Rearrange the words to form Jesus' great advice.

to to have
others you them you
Do do as would

D_____

_____

_____

That's the **golden rule**: treat people the same way you'd like them to treat you, no matter how they actually treat you.

Read verses 32-36

Get the picture? It's easy to be loving and generous to people who are the same to us. It's not so easy to be kind when you might get treated badly in return. But that's how Jesus wants His followers to live.

Why? **Because God has shown us so much love, even though we've treated Him so badly. He even sent His Son to die for us!** So we should show the same love to others.

Action!
Who treats you badly?

_____

_____

How can you show love and kindness to them this week?

_____

_____

_____

_____

Make sure to try it out!

Pray!

Ask God to help you be more like Him, showing love to those people you've just written down.

69

Don't judge or grudge

Luke 6 v 37-38

Jesus has been giving loads of great advice on how Christians should live to please God.

Next tip coming up...

> I hate Helen. She's always being nasty about people behind their backs!

We've probably all done that loads of times — criticised someone else when we're just as bad ourselves.

Read Luke 6 v 37

Crack the code for Jesus' words.

Don't be critical of other people or you can expect the same from them. And more importantly, GOD will treat you the same way.

Christians have had all their sins forgiven by God. So God expects them to forgive people who treat them badly.

Read verse 38

That's talking about someone being given a load of wheat! It means that if we treat other people well, God will reward us.

But we shouldn't be generous and forgiving just because there's a reward in it for us. We should treat people well because God has been so incredibly forgiving and generous to us!

Pray!

If you want to obey Jesus and treat people well, ask God to help you. Then make the effort to do it this week. Remember the Action! point from yesterday?

WEIRD WORDS

Condemn
Judge people, deciding that they deserve punishment

A	B	D	E	F	G	I	J	L	N	O	R	T	U	V	W	Y

10

Luke
6 v 39-42

Next, Jesus uses picture stories (parables) to give some more brilliant advice on how to live God's way.

WEIRD WORDS

Speck
Tiny amount

Hypocrite
Someone who says one thing, but does the opposite

Plank you very much

Read Luke 6 v 39

> **Picture 1**
> A b_____ person can't lead another blind p_____. They would both f_____ into a pit!

What's it mean?

The Pharisees were telling people how to live. But they were not living God's way themselves! So how could they teach other people? They were guiding people wrongly, like a blind person leading another blind person towards a deep pit!

Read verse 40

> **Picture 2**
> The student is not above the t_____, but everyone who is fully tr_____ will be like their t_____.

What's it mean?

We'll live like the people we learn from. So if we have unreliable teachers (like the Pharisees) we probably won't live God's way. But if we have people teaching us truthfully from the Bible, we're more likely to live God's way. **Learn from God's Word** and you'll start serving Him more!

Read verses 41-42

> **Picture 3**
> Why do you look at the s_____ of sawdust in your b_____ eye and ignore the plank in your own e_____?!

What's it mean?

Crazy, isn't it? We can see other people's tiny faults but ignore our own **ENORMOUS** ones.

We have to sort out our own sin problems first, before dishing out advice or criticism to others.

Action!

What faults of your own do you need to sort out?

_____

_____

_____

Pray!

Ask God to help you with those planks! And thank Him for people who teach you from the Bible.

71

Mission possible

Luke 9 v 1-9

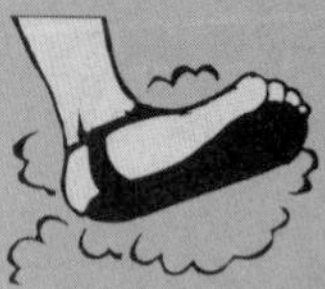

Jesus chose twelve men to learn from Him and tell people about Him.

WEIRD WORDS

The Twelve
The twelve disciples/ apostles

Demons
Evil spirits which made people ill

Staff
Big stick

Testimony
Evidence

Tetrarch
Ruler

Perplexed
Puzzled and confused

John
John the Baptist

Elijah
Prophet from Old Testament times

Flick back to Luke 6 v 12-16

… for a reminder of the men Jesus chose. Now we jump ahead a few chapters to see what Jesus has planned for them. *The missing words are all down the centre.*

Read Luke 9 v 1-2

Jesus gave the 12 disciples the p_________ to drive out d___________ and cure d_______________ (v1). He sent them to p___________ the k_____________ of God and to h________ the sick (v2).

Jesus sent them to tell people to live with God in charge of their lives. He gave them the power to heal people as a sign that God had sent them.

Read verses 3-6

He told them to take n_____________ with them (v3). No s_________, b____, b_________, m__________ or extra c____________ (v3). If people didn't w____________ them, they should shake d_______ from their f_______ (v5) as a sign that God was not pleased with those people.

bag
bread
clothes
demons
diseases
dust
feet
heal
kingdom
money
nothing
power
preach
proclaim
staff
welcome

They were not allowed to take possessions with them. It made them rely on God for everything. Everywhere they went, God provided them with food, clothes and somewhere to stay!

Think!

Do you trust God to give you everything you really need?
Is He the first person you turn to for help?

Read verses 7-9

Herod didn't know who Jesus was. In the next few days, we'll discover exactly who Jesus is and why He lived on earth.

Pray!

Thank God that He gives us the ability to serve Him and tell others about Him. Thank God that we can rely on Him for everything we need.

12

**Luke
9 v 10-17**

*Jesus is
spending time
alone with His
twelve disciples,
teaching and
encouraging
them.*

*But they're not
alone for very
long...*

Feeding five fousand

Read Luke 9 v 10-11

Jesus didn't tell them to get lost.
Instead, He welcomed the people
because He saw how much they
needed Him.

Wow!

Jesus never turns away people who
need Him. He welcomes them and
gives them what they need.

Read verses 12-15

1000s of people

+ **not much food**

+ **a long way from the shops**

= **A BIG PROBLEM!**

*How much food did the disciples
find?*

_____ **loaves of bread**

+ _____ **fish**

= **enough for a family picnic**

That's nowhere near enough to feed
thousands of people. But it's not a
problem for Jesus...

Read verses 16-17

Jesus is God's Son. Because of His
great love for these people, Jesus
did this incredible miracle and fed
them all! There were even twelve
baskets of scraps left over!

Wow!

NOTHING is impossible for Jesus!
That means even our biggest
problems are NO PROBLEM for
Jesus.

Think!

What problems do you have?

_____

_____

_____

_____

Pray!

Jesus is God's Son. You can take
your problems to Jesus right
now and ask Him to help you
with them.

Who is Jesus?

**Luke
9 v 18-22**

People were amazed by Jesus.

He did incredible miracles, healed people and said astonishing things.

They wondered who He was.

WEIRD WORDS

John the Baptist
The man who had prepared the way for Jesus and baptised Him

Elijah
Old Testament prophet

Messiah/Christ
God's chosen Rescuer

Read Luke 9 v 18-19

Fill in some of the people's ideas about Jesus (v19).

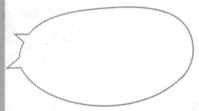

So Jesus asked His disciples a very important question...

Who do YOU say I am?

Read verses 20-21

Fill in Peter's answer.

It might sound obvious to us, but it was actually an amazing answer!

Wow! 1

For years, the Jewish people had been expecting THE MESSIAH (the Christ), who was promised in the Old Testament, to come and save them.

Now Peter was saying that **Jesus** was the great Messiah sent by God!

Read what Jesus said would happen to Him in verse 22

Now read it again!

Wow! 2

Jesus was the Messiah who came to save His people. So He had to suffer and be killed to take the punishment people deserve for disobeying God.

Wow! 3

Then Jesus was raised back to life! He beat death, so that if we trust Him to forgive us, we can live with Him forever in eternal life!

Pray!

Read slowly through verse 22, thanking Jesus for each of the things He went through so that you could have your sins forgiven by God.

Hard to follow

What do you think living as a Christian involves?

_____
_____
_____
_____
_____

Let's see if Jesus agrees...

Read Luke 9 v 23-27

Fill in the vowels to reveal what a follower of Jesus must do.

1. Deny th__ms__lv__s (v23)

That means stop putting yourself first. Christians have Jesus in charge of their lives. So they live to please Him, not themselves.

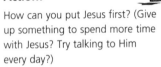

Action!

How can you put Jesus first? (Give up something to spend more time with Jesus? Try talking to Him every day?)

_____
_____
_____

3. Whoever is ash__m__d of me and my w__rds, I will be __sh__m__d of th__m (v26)

Jesus let Himself be killed so He could rescue us! We shouldn't be embarrassed about Him — He's the best thing that has happened to us!

Action!

How will you show people you're not ashamed of Jesus?

_____
_____
_____
_____

WEIRD WORDS

Disciple
Follower

Forfeit
Give up

Son of Man
Jesus

Comes in his glory
Everyone will see how awesome and perfect Jesus is

2. T__ke up their cr__ss d__ily and f__ll__w m__ (v23)

Jesus carried His cross on His way to die in our place. And He expects His followers to be prepared to die for Him!

Most of us won't have to die for our faith in Jesus, but we will face tough times for telling people about Jesus.

Pray!

Thank Jesus for dying in your place. Ask Him to help you live your life for Him, doing the things you've written under Action!

**Luke
9 v 28-36**

*Ever stood on top
of a mountain?*

*The view is
spectacular.*

*Peter, John
and James saw
something even
more amazing
at the top of this
mountain...*

WEIRD WORDS

**Glorious
splendour**
Impressive brilliance!

Departure
Jesus' death and
resurrection

Enveloped
Completely
surrounded

Glowing report

Read Luke 9 v 28-31

*Fill in the missing Es, Ts and Cs to
show what they saw.*

**1. The app__aran__e of
Jesus' fa__e __hang__d
and his __lo__hes be__am__
dazzlingly brigh__**

Wow! They got to see how
awesome and **impressive** Jesus
really is.

**2. __lijah and Mos__s
__alk__d wi__h J__sus**

Theses were two great men who
served God in Old Testament times.
But Jesus is far greater than even
these two! Jesus is God's Son.

Read verses 32-33

Peter was so scared, he blurted
out the first thing that came into
his head! But someone else had
something to say...

Read verses 34-36

The voice in the cloud was God
Himself! *What did He say (v35)?*

**__his is my Son whom I
hav__ __hos__n. Lis__en
__o Him.**

Jesus really is God's Son. God wants
us to listen to Jesus.

Wow!

- That means reading more about
Jesus in the Bible

- Staying awake and listening in
church and youth meetings

- It also means acting on what
we learn

Action!

Here's a way to help you listen and
learn from what Jesus says. Grab
a notebook and rename it your
"Jesus File". Split each page up
like the example below. Every time
you read about Jesus in the Bible or
hear about Him in a meeting, fill in
a page.

Bible passage:

**What it says about Jesus or
what Jesus teaches**

What I've learned

**What I'm going to do
about it**

Pray!

Ask God to help you to listen
to Jesus and to learn from what
He says.

Can you believe it?

**Luke
9 v 37-45**

After the amazing thing that happened on the mountain (see yesterday's Discover), Jesus comes down to chaos...

WEIRD WORDS

Spirit/Demon
Evil spirit

Convulsions
Shaking wildly

Perverse
Disobedient to God

Rebuked
Commanded it to leave the boy alone

Read Luke 9 v 37-40

Cross out the wrong answers.

A man/woman/gerbil called out to Jesus to help his son/moon/stars (v38).
An evil sprite/spirit was in the boy, causing him to scream/shout/giggle and foam at the nose/mouth/ears (v39). It was destroying him. But the disciples/discover readers couldn't drive out the spirit (v40).

Read verse 41

Jesus called them **unbelieving**. The disciples had not trusted God to heal the boy. And the people still did not believe that Jesus was God's Son who had come to rescue them.

Think!

What about you? Do you believe that Jesus is God's Son? Have you trusted Him to rescue you from sin?

Read verses 42-43

The demon threw the boy to the sky/ground/gravy but Jesus shook/healed the boy and the angel/demon left him (v42). Everyone was amazed/bored at the greatness of God (v43).

Think!

Are you amazed at how great God is?! Spend time making a list of some of the great things about God.

Read verses 43-45

Jesus told His disciples that He would be betrayed and handed over to men (who would kill Him). But they didn't understand what Jesus was talking about.

Pray!

Ask God to help you **understand** why Jesus had to die.
Ask God to help you **believe** that Jesus is God's Son.
Then spend time **praising** God for how great and powerful and loving He is.

Serving suggestions

Do you ever boast about stuff?

Or try to prove that you're better than someone else?

That's what the disciples were doing...

WEIRD WORDS

Resolutely
With great determination

Samaritan
In Samaria, an area where Jews were hated

Rebuked
Told off

Read Luke 9 v 46-48

*Cross out the **X**s to reveal what Jesus said.*

XWHXXOXEXVEXRX
XWEXLCOXMEXSTHIXSLXI
TXTXLEXCHXXILXDINMXY
NAXMEXWEXLCOMXESMEX

W_____
_____
_____
_____

Back then, kids were considered unimportant. They had no rights and no education. We should be welcoming to people who are worse off or weaker than us. It's like welcoming Jesus Himself!

Action!

I will be more friendly to

_____

(Write the name of an elderly person or someone at school)

Read verses 49-50

John thought that only the twelve disciples could serve Jesus in a special way.

But Jesus disagreed.

What did He say?

XWHOXEXVEXRIXSNX
XOXTAXXGAXIXNSXTYXX
OXUIXXSFOXRXYOXXUXX

W_____
_____
_____

Do you ever think you're better than other Christians? If they're serving God too, then show them love and support!

Action!

I will be more supportive to

_____

even though we disagree about stuff.

Read verses 51-56

These people wouldn't welcome Jesus because they hated Jews. James and John wanted to destroy the village but Jesus told them off.

Pray!

Do you actually mean the things you've written in the Action! sections? Ask God to help you put them into practice.

78

Luke
9 v 57-62

So, you still want to follow Jesus?

Maybe we should try to put you off the idea...

Follow the leader

Read Luke 9 v 57-58

I'll follow you wherever you go!

Draw pictures to complete Jesus' answer to him (v58).

have dens

and have nests

but the Son of Man has nowhere to lay his

Jesus was saying that it's not easy following Him. There are lots of things you have to give up.

Think!

Do you want to be a follower of Jesus? DON'T ANSWER!

Not until you've considered how hard a Christian's life can be and what living for Jesus would mean for your life.

Read verses 59-62

These people wanted to follow Jesus... but only after they had gone to a funeral or said goodbye to their family. Jesus' answer sounds harsh...

Let the spiritually dead people who don't serve God bury the dead (v60). Anyone who puts other things ahead of serving God isn't fit to serve Him (v62).

Wow!

If we're serious about following Jesus, then NOTHING will be more important to us than Him.

Think!

What things sometimes become more important to you than serving God?

_____

_____

_____

Pray!

Following Jesus is hard!! Ask God to help you stick at it, and put Jesus FIRST in your life.

79

Joshua: Follow the leader

Let's get back to Joshua to see how he and the Israelites are doing at conquering Canaan — the land God promised them.

WEIRD WORDS

The Jordan
Huge river

Ruse
Deceiving trick

Delegation
Group of people

Wineskins
Wine bottles made of animal skin

Treaty
Peace agreement

Hivites
Gibeonites

Joshua and the Israelites had just destroyed the city of Ai.

Their enemies heard the news...

Read Joshua 9 v 1-2

But before Joshua was able to make his battle plans, some weird-looking people showed up.

Read verses 3-13

In the box below, draw what these people looked like. If you're rubbish at drawing, just make a list of the weird things about them.

[ ]

These guys were conmen out to trick Joshua. They lived in Canaan but pretended to be from far away to escape being destroyed by the Israelites.

The Israelites were suspicious. God had been very clear that they **must not make treaties** with people in Canaan. Would they obey God's instruction, or give in to these guys?

Action!

God makes it clear to us too. Christians should obey Him and not compromise. If we know a particular thing is wrong, we must have nothing to do with it. *What things do you do that disobey God?*

_____

_____

_____

_____

Pray!

Ask God to help you to obey Him and not compromise. Ask Him to help you fight the temptation to do wrong.

Tomorrow, we'll find out where Joshua and the Israelites went wrong...

80

Joshua
9 v 14-21

The Gibeonites are pretending to be from a faraway country so that the Israelites make peace with them.

WEIRD WORDS

Sampled their provisions
Tried their food

Enquire
Ask

Ratified it by oath
Promised to stick to it

Wrath
God's anger and punishment

Trick or treaty

War and peace

- The Gibeonites asked for a peace treaty — for the Israelites to promise not to attack them.

- But God had told the Israelites not to make peace with His enemies in Canaan, including the Gibeonites.

- In fact, they should have nothing to do with them!

Read Deuteronomy 7 v 1-6

The Hivites (v1) are the same people as the Gibeonites!

Why did God command His people not to have anything to do with these nations (v4)?

_____

_____

_____

These Israelites were God's special people (v6) and other nations, like the Gibeonites, would turn them away from God.

So what did Joshua do?

Read Joshua 9 v 14-21

Joshua fell for the Gibeonites' story and made peace with them.

What big mistake did the Israelites make (v14)?

They did not _____

_____

Sometimes things look right, feel right, and seem to make sense: but they are actually **wrong**. The only way we can be sure is to **trust what God says**, even if it seems weird.

Don't be fooled like Joshua was. If you're unsure about anything, turn to God in prayer and ask Him to help you. And see what the Bible says. And ask an older Christian too.

Action!

On a sheet of paper, copy out Proverbs 3 v 5. You might want to decorate it, so it catches your eye. Stick it on your wall to remind you always to turn to God when you're not sure of something.

Off the hook

**Joshua
9 v 22-27**

*The Gibeonites
have tricked
Joshua and the
Israelites into
making a peace
treaty with them.*

*How will Joshua
react?*

Read Joshua 9 v 22-23

Joshua is furious with the Gibeonites
for tricking him.

*Unjumble the anagrams to reveal
what he said to them.*

You will always

have to be _____
S A L E V S

to the Israelites,

cutting _____ **and**
O D O W

carrying _____ .
E T R A W

But why had they lied to him?

Read verses 24-25

We heard that the

_____ **your** _____
D R O L   **O G D**

had given you the whole

_____ **of Canaan,**
N A L D

and told you to _____
I L K L

everyone who lived there.

We lied because we

_____ **for our lives.**
R E A F E D

The people from Gibeon are scared
of God and His people, the Israelites.

But they are still **God's enemies**
who deserve to be wiped out for
going against Him.

What will happen to them?

Read verses 26-27

God spared them! They became part
of His people!

Wow!

- If you're a Christian, then God has
  done the same for you!

- You've disobeyed Him and lived as
  His enemy: living for yourself and
  not for Him.

- You deserved to be punished by
  God.

- Yet He has forgiven you, and
  made you one of His people!

Pray!

Even though we've treated God
so badly, He gives us the chance
to be part of His special people!
You'd better get thanking Him...

Save the servants

**Joshua
10 v 1-7**

*Joshua and the
Israelites are
obeying God
and trying to
conquer the
land of Canaan.*

*That means
fighting battles
and destroying
cities.*

News travels fast. Five powerful
kings heard that Joshua had made a
peace treaty with the Gibeonites. So
they decided to attack Gibeon for
joining their enemy.

Read Joshua 10 v 1-5

*Complete the names of the kings by
filling in the missing vowels.*

P__r__m
(King of J__rm__th)

__d__n__ - Z__d__k
(King of J__r__s__l__m)

H__h__m
(King of H__br__n)

J__ph__ __
(King of L__ch__sh)

D__b__r
(King of __gl__n)

Why were they so concerned about
the city of Gibeon?

Read verses 6-7

How did the Gibeonites react?

**They asked
J__sh__ __ for h__lp**

What did Joshua do?

**M__rch__d to G__b__ __n
with his __rmy including
the b__st f__ghters**

The Gibeonites didn't deserve help,
did they? They had tricked the
Israelites into trusting them. But
Joshua didn't abandon them. He
stuck to his promise.

Wow!

We don't deserve Jesus' help.
Certainly not after the way we've
sinned against Him.

But Jesus never abandons those who
turn to Him.

Pray!

Lord, I've messed up loads of
times. Thank you so much for
never giving up on me and always
being there.

83

**Joshua
10 v 7-11**

*Five kings and
their armies are
attacking the
city of Gibeon.*

*Joshua and the
Israelites had
promised to
protect Gibeon,
so they're
marching out
to defend the
city...*

Hail to the king

They're up against five armies! Do
they stand a chance?

Read Joshua 10 v 7-8

*Rearrange the words to show what
God says to Joshua.*

_____

_____

_____

of   not   afraid

them   Do   be

_____

_____

_____

_____

one   be   able   you

against   of   to   will

Not   them   stand

**God is on their side! He will
give them the victory! They
can rely on Him!**

Read verses 9-11

Who gave the Israelites victory?

┌─────────────────────────┐
│   │
│   │
│   │
└─────────────────────────┘

It was **God** who panicked the
enemy (v10). And **God** who chased
them with hailstones (v11).

Think!

What difficult situations do you face
in life? (Hassle from friends? Trouble
at home?)

_____

_____

_____

_____

Read Hebrews 13 v 6

Wow!

If you're a believer, God tells you
not to be afraid. He is fighting
on your side, helping you battle
through the troubles that life throws
at you!

Pray!

Do you need to ask God to help
you? And thank Him for fighting
on your side?

Sun stopper

**Joshua
10 v 12-15**

*Joshua and the
Israelites are
fighting the
massive armies
of the Amorites.*

*And God is
fighting on
their side,
giving them
a spectacular
victory!*

WEIRD WORDS

Avenged itself
Got revenge

Book of Jashar
Book about Israel's
history, especially
the wars the
Israelites fought

Read Joshua 10 v 12-13

*Complete Joshua's prayer by
drawing pictures in the boxes.*

Make the

stand still over Gibeon

and the

**stand still over the Valley of
Aijalon until we've defeated
our enemies.**

God did just as Joshua asked, and
the Israelites won the battle against
their enemies.

The sun and moon standing still for
a whole day is pretty spectacular.
But it's not the most amazing thing
that happened that day...

Read verses 14-15

The most incredible thing was that
the Lord listened to a human being!
The King of heaven and earth
listened to Joshua and answered his
prayer!

Action!

Make a list of what God is like.
Psalm 147 will give you some ideas.

_____

_____

_____

_____

_____

_____

Think!

Before you pray every day, look
at your list to remind you exactly
who you're praying to: the King of
Heaven!

Pray!

Thank the Lord that even
though He is the awesome King
of Heaven, He listens to your
prayers! Tell Him what's on your
mind right now.

85

Joshua
10 v 16-27

With God's help, the Israelites have been fighting against five evil kings and their armies.

Cowardly cave kings

Most of the armies had been destroyed, but the five kings were still on the run...

Read Joshua 10 v 16-21

... and answer these questions.

Where were the five kings hiding out?

Behind a very large wall ☐

In a cave at Makkedah ☐

In a cave at Macclesfield ☐

What were Joshua's instructions to his men?

Roll large socks up to the mouth of the cave ☐

Roll large rocks up to the mouth of the cake ☐

Roll large rocks up to the mouth of the cave ☐

These five kings were God's...

Friends ☐

Enemies ☐

Worshippers ☐

God had sentenced these kings and their people to destruction. Over the years, they had continued to sin against God. They deserved His punishment.

Read verses 22-27

What did Joshua tell his army commanders to do?

Put their necks on the feet of the kings ☐

Put the kings on the necks of their feet ☐

Put their feet on the necks of the kings ☐

Doing this showed that the Israelites had **conquered** these enemies.

Look at verse 25 again

Wow!

That must have been so encouraging for the Israelites! God promises to conquer all of His people's enemies like that!

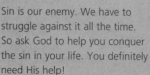

Pray!

Sin is our enemy. We have to struggle against it all the time. So ask God to help you conquer the sin in your life. You definitely need His help!

**Joshua
10 v 28-43**

God has commanded Joshua and the Israelites to invade and conquer the land of Canaan.

Taste of victory

God had promised to give this land to the Israelites. Now this promise was coming true...

Read Joshua 10 v 28-30

All of today's answers can be found in the wordsearch.

T	D	L	F	M	D	R	O	L
L	I	B	N	A	H	S	M	Y
A	D	R	E	K	V	V	P	U
C	N	L	A	K	J	H	K	L
H	U	O	J	E	H	E	K	O
I	T	R	L	D	E	B	I	R
S	Q	D	F	A	D	R	O	D
H	N	E	R	H	Z	O	C	B
C	B	E	G	L	O	N	G	O

Which two cities did Joshua and the Israelites conquer?

M_____

and L_____

It sounds horrible, but these people deserved this punishment for going against God.

Who gave Joshua the victory? (v30)

The L_____

Read verses 31-35

Which cities were next?

L_____

and E_____

Who gave them the victory? (v32)

The L_____

Read verses 36-43

Which two other cities did Joshua and the Israelites conquer?

H_____

and D_____

That's a lot of victories for one army!

Who won these victories for the Israelites? (v42)

The L_____

They couldn't have done it without the Lord fighting for them.

Wow!

Christians have many battles in life — tough times, temptation, hassle from friends, family problems and other stuff. The brilliant news is that God is always fighting for His people.

Pray!

Want to spend some time talking to this awesome God? Tell Him what's on your mind, and ask Him to help.

Northern fights

**Joshua
11 v 1-15**

God is giving the entire land of Canaan to the Israelites.

But they've got to drive out all the godless people who live there.

They've defeated all the armies in the south.

But what about the ones in the north?

WEIRD WORDS

Slain
Killed

Hamstring
Cripple them

Plunder and livestock
Treasure and animals

Jabin, the most powerful northern king, heard about the Israelites winning many battles. So he gathered all the other kings and armies in northern Canaan to fight against Joshua and the Israelites.

Read Joshua 11 v 1-5

This was a MASSIVE army for the Israelites to fight!

How many men were in it?

As many as the

_____ **on the**

_____ **(v4)**

How could God's people stand a chance against this vast army?!

Read verse 6

> **Do not**
> _____ **of**
> **them. Tomorrow, I will**
> _____
> _____
> _____ **Israel**

God was on their side, fighting for them!

Read verses 7-8

Who gave them the victory? (v8)

[ ]

Read verses 9-15

• God even told Joshua how to win this impossible battle.

• The Israelites didn't have any horses or chariots, so God told them how to beat the enemies' horses and chariots!

• The Israelites attacked the enemy in their camp before they could use their chariots in battle.

• Joshua did exactly as the Lord commanded him (v15).

Action!

On a sheet of paper, write HOW CAN I OBEY GOD TODAY? in huge letters. Stick it on your wall. Every day, look at it and think how you can obey what you've read in the Bible recently. Then do it!

88

War and peace

**Joshua
11 v 16-23**

*God had
promised to
give the land
of Canaan to
His people, the
Israelites.*

And God kept His promise! He helped Joshua and the Israelites defeat all the godless people in Canaan so they could live there.

But it wasn't easy for them...

Read Joshua 11 v 16-18

It doesn't take us long to read about their victories. But it took them **over 5 years** of horrible blood-filled battles! Living for God takes hard work and patience.

Fill in the vowels (aeiou) to complete **Hebrews 10 v 36**.

> Y__ __ n__ __d t__
> p__rs__rv__r__

That means be patient, keep going! Keep serving God! It won't always be easy, but you must keep going.

Read Joshua 11 v 19-20

What did God do to His enemies?

> H__rd__n__d th__ __r
> h__ __rts (v20)

These people turned against God, worshipped idols and did all kinds of horrific things. God hardened their hearts so they couldn't turn to Him, and then they were destroyed.

They got the punishment they deserved. God was in complete control.

Read verses 21-23

Who else did Joshua defeat?

> The A_____ (v21)

These were giant people who had terrified the Israelites years earlier. They thought even God couldn't destroy them.

But now we see that God did destroy them!

Pray!

God is in complete control. Thank the Lord that He is powerful enough to help us face our most terrifying fears.
What are you most afraid of? Talk to God about it.

WEIRD WORDS

Exterminating
Killing everyone

Without mercy
No chance of being let off

Tribal divisions
The Israelites were divided into 12 different tribes

Conquering kings

Joshua 12 v 1-24

Today's Bible bit looks like a boring list of boring kings.

But God's got loads to tell us...

DEBIRGEDERMADONHAZORJERICHOAILIBNAHADULLAM
JARMUTHLACHISHTAANACHMEGIDDOTAPPUAHHEPHER
HORMAHARADMAKKEDAHBETHELJERUSALEMHEBRON
EGLONGEZERSHIMRONMERONAKSHAPHAPHEK
LASHARONTIRZAHKEDESHJOKNEAMDORGOYIM

This may look like a load of nonsense, but it's the names of the 31 places that the Israelites conquered. Put lines between the end of each name and the start of the next one to separate them. Use **Joshua 12 v 7-24** to help you.

But this isn't a dull, dreary list. It shows all the places in Canaan that God conquered for His people. It shows that He kept His promise to give them the land of Canaan! It shows how incredibly powerful God is! He conquered all these kings!

Now read verses 1-6

God defeated Kings Sihon and Og too.

> They lived **outside** of Canaan. So why are they mentioned?

> Because some of the Israelites were allowed to live **outside** of Canaan, where these two kings used to rule.

King Sihon

King Og

WEIRD WORDS

Territory
Land

Even though they lived outside of Canaan, they were still part of God's people, the Israelites.

It's easy to look down on Christians who are different from you. (Maybe they worship God differently, or look weird, or get on your nerves.)

But they are still **part of God's people**.

Pray!

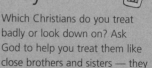

Which Christians do you treat badly or look down on? Ask God to help you treat them like close brothers and sisters — they are God's children too!

God's great gifts

God helped the Israelites conquer Canaan. Next, God dished out different areas of Canaan for the different Israelite tribes to live in...

Read Joshua 13 v 1-7

Joshua was old and doddery, but there were still large areas of Canaan to be conquered and enemy armies to defeat.

Cross out the Xs, As and Ks to reveal what God promised (v6).

AXIWAXILAXALD

RAXKXIVXAKETAXKH

KEXKAAMKOAXKUXAT

I _____

_____

God always keeps His promises. **Nothing** can stand in His way.

The rest of this chapter lists the places which God gave to some of the Israelite tribes.

Skim read verses 8-32

In the verses, find...

• **a town beginning with J:**

J_____

• **a mountain:**

_____

• **a town beginning with S:**

S_____

This looks like an unexciting list, but it was sooo encouraging for the Israelites. And for us too...

Wow!

It reminds us of all the places God conquered for His people and of all the battles He won. It reminds us that God is in control and that He keeps His promises!

God gave parts of Canaan to all of the tribes except one.

Read verse 33

The tribe of Levi didn't inherit land. They inherited **God** Himself!

They got to serve Him and they would get to live with Him forever!

Pray!

Read that last paragraph again. It's true for ALL of God's people — Christians. If you're one of God's people, thank Him for this great gift.

Caleb's courage

Joshua 14 v 1-9

It's time to meet one of the unsung heroes of Israel.

But first, there's more land to dish out...

WEIRD WORDS

Allotted
Gave

Assigned by lot
Threw dice to help them decide who would live in each area

Pasture-lands
Places for their animals to graze

Convictions
What he really believed

Read Joshua 14 v 1-5

Next, an old guy called Caleb shows up and claims that he should get some of the land for himself. Time-waster or hero?

Read verses 6-9

What's he jabbering on about?

Time for a recap...

Years ago, Moses sent twelve spies into Canaan to report on it before the Israelites invaded it.

Ten of them gave exaggerated reports that Canaan had terrifying giants, huge cities and that it couldn't be conquered.

 +

Only Joshua and Caleb told the truth. They knew that God would give them victory in Canaan.

But the people believed the ten spineless spies.

They disobeyed God and refused to go into Canaan.

Caleb stood up against everyone else, and trusted in God. For showing courage, God promised to take Caleb into Canaan and give him land. (You can find the whole story in Numbers chapters 13 and 14.)

Being a Christian and obeying God can be tough, even lonely at times. Standing up for what is right can be unpopular.

Think!

What specific things might YOU have to do, to make a stand for God? (eg: refusing to cheat, disagreeing when friends disrespect the Bible)

_____

_____

_____

_____

_____

Pray!

Ask God to help you make a stand for Him — to give you the courage to trust Him and live for Him. Maybe there are specific situations you need to ask help with.

Senior strength

**Joshua
14 v 10-15**

*Old man Caleb
has asked
Joshua to
give him the
land that God
promised him
years ago.*

WEIRD WORDS

Vigorous
Full of strength.
Up for it!

Anakites
A people famous
for being huge
and scary!

Fortified
Well-protected

Read Joshua 14 v 10-11

*What did 85 year-old Caleb say?
Cross out the **B**s **C**s and **F**s.*

BIMACSSTFFROBFNG

TOCCDABYASFCIWAFBS

45YCEAFRSBBACGO!B

I'M_____

_____

_____

What else?

FTHBCELBOFRDCCHAS

BKECFPTMFFEALBIVCE

_____

_____

_____

Caleb was looking back on his life
and remembering how good God
had been to him.

Think!

How has God been good to you?

_____

_____

_____

_____

_____

Never forget what God has done for
you in your life!

Read verses 12-15

Caleb asked Joshua for the hill
country where the huge Anakites
lived. He was 85 years old, and he
wanted to fight giants!

What did he say (v12)?

FWITBHTCCHEBFLOB

RDCHELPCCFBINGCM

BEIFWILBLDFBRIVCE

TBBHEFFFMOCUTB

W_____

_____

_____

_____

It didn't matter that Caleb was 85.
He knew he could trust God to do
the seemingly impossible and keep
His promise.

Pray!

Read yesterday's Think! section.
Ask God to help you to trust
Him to be with you as you stand
up for Him. And thank Him for
the things you wrote in today's
Think! section.

Next issue, we continue the Israelites' story in the book of Judges.

DISCOVER
COLLECTION

DISCOVER ISSUE 10

Meet heroes and villains in the book of Judges. Listen in on tremendous teaching from Jesus in Luke. Learn about God's unstoppable love in Romans. And get your heart in tune as we explore Psalms.

ISSUE 10

COLLECT 12 THE SET

COLLECT ALL 12 ISSUES TO COMPLETE THE DISCOVER COLLECTION

Don't forget to order the next issue of Discover. Or even better, grab a one-year subscription to make sure Discover lands in your hands as soon as it's out. Packed full of puzzles, prayers and pondering points.

thegoodbook.co.uk thegoodbook.com

thegoodbook COMPANY